T

The University of Georgia Press ATHENS & LONDON

The Measured Word

ON POETRY AND SCIENCE

Edited by Kurt Brown

WITH AN INTRODUCTION BY ALBERT GOLDBARTH

© 2001 by the University of Georgia Press
Athens, Georgia 30602
All rights reserved

Acknowledgment of previously published material
appears on pages 203–4

Designed by Erin Kirk New
Set in 10.5 on 13 Minion
Printed and bound by McNaughton & Gunn

The paper in this book meets the guidelines for
permanence and durability of the Committee on
Production Guidelines for Book Longevity of the
Council on Library Resources.

Printed in the United States of America

05 04 03 02 01 C 5 4 3 2 1

05 04 03 02 01 P 5 4 3 2 1

Library of Congress Cataloging-in-Publication Data

The measured word : on poetry and science / edited by Kurt
Brown, with an introduction by Albert Goldbarth.
    p. cm.
Includes bibliographical references.
ISBN 0-8203-2286-5 (alk. paper) —ISBN 0-8203-2287-3 (pbk. :
alk. paper)
1. Poetry—History and criticism. 2. Literature and science.
    I. Brown, Kurt.
PN1083.S43 M43 2001
809.1′9356—dc21   00-045133

British Library Cataloging-in-Publication Data available

To the memory of Miroslav Holub
citizen of both cultures

Contents

Introduction

Perhaps the arts and the sciences have never slept together without one eye kept warily open. By now, however, our common understanding in this age of specialization (and therefore fragmentation) is that, in some idyllic past, the sciences and the arts were at peace, were one.

Is this a *myth*, a oneness seen as an Edenic park where lion and lamb, field mouse and snake haven't reached differentiation yet and romp together? Or is it a *fact*, at least in the sense in which most readers of this book will assume that the Hawkingesque ur-universe is a "fact": an endlessly heavy dot of holistic existence, where everything (matter *and* energy, the street mime *and* the Rutgers astrophysicist) coexists equally?

In either case, it isn't very difficult to imagine back to a world in which the "artisan" creating the black and bisque-red beasts that charge across the walls of Altamira and Lascaux is one half of the happily mingled unity in which the other half, the clan's "technician," invents new ways of turning the earth into a palette of useful pigments. This is the feeling—one of partnership—we receive when reading about the English Romantic poets. Shelley conducted gassy, frizzling, eggy chemical experiments (historian Paul Johnson says "his *Witch of Atlas*, with energy supplied by electricity and magnetism, is the earliest great poem of space travel"); and Mary Shelley knew enough about the serious eighteenth- and nineteenth-century biology lab (Galvani, Erasmus Darwin) to dream its research into her grand, albeit cautionary, *Frankenstein*. Wordsworth says the poet "will be ready to follow the steps of the man of science. . . . He will be at his side, carrying sensation into the midst of the objects of the science itself. The remotest discoveries of the chemist, the botanist, or mineralogist will be as proper objects of the poet's art as any."

Coleridge worked with Humphry Davy (who was "already regarded as Britain's leading scientist") in early protophotography attempts to fix an image. They exchanged a correspondence on the effect of nitrous oxide (Coleridge: "I could not avoid . . . beating the ground with my feet; and after the mouth-piece was removed, I remained for a few seconds motionless, in great extacy"). Peter Roget of *Roget's Thesaurus* fame also experimented with nitrous oxide as part of Davy's investigations; so did Robert Southey, whose gas-induced visions of paradise were later part of his poem *The Curse of Kehama*. For his part, Davy read Kant, at Coleridge's urging, and wrote poems: Southey published some in 1799, and at one time Davy had plans for an epic poem on the life of Moses.

But if this *was* a version of Eden, we were expelled; or, if it *was* a Hawkingesque primordial dot, it exploded to slivers. At a meeting with Humphry Davy (by then Sir Humphry Davy) in 1827, it was obvious to Wordsworth that two languages were being spoken, neither side with a key to the other's tongue. "His scientific pursuits had hurried his mind into a course where I could not follow him, and had diverted it in proportion from objects with which I was best acquainted."

Eighteen twenty-seven was also the year Blake died; his poems and paintings exhibit a heated, lifelong grumble against the work of

Newton, its logic, its willingness to explore by ruler and calipers. Later in that century, the speaker of Whitman's "When I Heard the Learn'd Astronomer" storms out "tired and sick" from the lecture room, preferring "the mystical moist night-air" to "figures, . . . charts and diagrams." ("Derogation," Marty Williams calls this in his essay included here, and he's right: Whitman is in high dudgeon.)

And this is also the cultural moment when, in counterbalance, scientists turn their backs on the practitioners of the art of their day. By the time of the Armory Show in 1913, European and American visual art (*and* music *and* literature) exists on its side of a formidable divide. There's no Rosetta stone by which the explosive energy of *Nude Descending a Staircase* can be deciphered as a recognizable body to the biologist of 1913.

And so we've reached what C. P. Snow has famously termed (as Kelly Cherry's essay aptly reminds us) "the two cultures." Even so, there have always been those whose spirits are willing to bridge that chasm.

Jacob Bronowski is a fine example, and sturdily serves as epigraph-provider for Alison Deming's "Science and Poetry: A View from the Divide." Grumble over Newton though he did, Blake had a vision that was arguably an experiment in cosmology; so it isn't completely surprising that Bronowski, one of our century's most able and popular chroniclers of the history of science (his TV series *The Ascent of Man* is one grandiloquent scientific cheer), was also a serious student of Blake's work: an image by Blake is the cover art for Bronowski's *The Origins of Knowledge and Imagination*. Perhaps this can prepare us for Stephanie Strickland's savvy essay wherein that great naysayer-to-science William Blake is invoked (along with Emily Dickinson) as a paver-of-the-way for this century's hypertexts.

In fact, what we have in *The Measured Word* is a treasury of chasm-bridgers. Some are clearly enthusiasts: matchmakers pairing up science and art. Others are clearly more like reporters sent to cover a border skirmish ("Poetry and science are opposed, even hostile, enterprises," Emily Grosholz declares at the start of her essay; she'll end it by using the word "engagement," and we're reminded how both lovers *and* armies are said to "engage"). Jonathan Holden considers the fruitful interface of poetry and mathematics. Pattiann Rogers explores the ways in which miracles and forms of worship can flower in the fields of physics. Miroslav Holub concludes that a "hard-centered scientific approach" and a "soft-centered artistic approach" achieve "a total amalgamation" in the context of . . . but I won't spoil the punch of his observation here.

Nor should I natter on, while the essays themselves await you: bright, in some ways I'd say *necessary*, essays. Because when Humphry Davy and company were floating in nitrous oxide, they experienced the wholeness of existence, felt its disparate elements come together to make a Singularity, an All. That may be true or not true, but we owe it to ourselves at least to map such possibilities. Or we may as well give up on that essential term, the *uni*-verse.

THE MEASURED WORD

Twentieth-Century Cosmology and the Soul's Habitation

I'm very curious about the grid upon which we mentally place ourselves in time and space. There must be a grid of some kind there for each of us, a visual scaffolding, for balance, for orientation. Where and how do we envision ourselves located in time and space? Born in a certain year? At a certain location? By calendar? By map?

But is there more than that in our vision? Do we establish shapes and patterns that form boundaries of history and place inside of which we see ourselves and by which we define ourselves? Do we have an underlying conception of our spatial location in the world when we are out walking, or traveling by air, or inside our homes, here and now? What exactly is the "here and now" for our culture? And does this placing of ourselves in the universe affect our structure of moral values, the way we order our experiences, the way we explain our origins to ourselves?

They must be related. What does it mean to our image of family, landscape, art, to believe that light travels at a constant speed, that light falling through the forest at this moment left the surface of the sun nine minutes before, or that when we look up into the stars we are seeing back through billions of years? What a strange conception—that light carries not only knowledge but time and distance as well.

What exactly is our cosmology, then, the cosmology of our culture today, and how much does it affect our thinking? Does our cosmology permeate the language in subtle ways, the language then structuring our perceptions? These are questions of interest to me, and I don't have all the answers to them.

I'm going to define cosmology as the story of the universe, the explanation of the origin and history and processes of the universe, an explanation that creates the structure upon which we locate ourselves and define ourselves in relation to the objects we observe around us, and by which we also address our own origins and our nature.

Edward R. Harrison, in *Cosmology: The Science of the Universe*, states the importance of cosmology in this way:

> Every society creates universes; not only do these universes reflect the societies, but each universe controls the history and destiny of its society. The most powerful and influential ideas in any society are those that relate to the universe; they shape history, inspire civilizations, foment wars, create empires and establish political systems.

Previous cultures have invented a variety of cosmologies. Some have told stories of magic, stories that explained everything by the motives and actions of ambient spirits inhabiting the natural world and fashioned in the image of humankind. The cosmology of mythology constructed a universe in which the spirits of magic retreated and became remote gods. Anthropocentric cosmologies pictured human beings at the center of the universe, above the beasts, occupying a place of importance, next to the angels, possessing the attention of the creator of all things. During the Middle Ages cosmology and religion were one.

But according to Harrison, "No persons living in the twentieth century can claim to be educated if they are unaware of the *modern* vision of the physical universe and the history of the magnificent concepts that it embodies."

I do believe that the cosmology of our times is at the root of much of what we write and the attitudes and values we espouse, whether we are completely aware of it or not. The world picture we hold today has for the most part been given to us by science, and all of us believe it, to some degree, and even more important, whether we declare we believe in it or not, we act on it, base decisions on it, live by it, and demonstrate daily our faith in it.

I want to state very briefly and simply the way I believe many of us visualize the universe and our place in it, the way I, as a layperson, understand our cosmology. Most of us are so accustomed to these ideas that they may seem ordinary and unsurprising, which proves my contention that this is the cosmology of our time, held closely by the members of our community.

We see ourselves as very tiny beings made up physically of groupings of other even tinier entities, atoms, molecules, cells, and organs. We are made from the dust of old stars. Most of us believe we have risen through natural selection and mutation of genes over many, many millions of years, our bodies being related to all other living bodies on Earth. Beautiful and fine, lovely story, invigorating and incorporating theory, in my opinion.

And we see ourselves as very tiny beings relative to the size of Earth, our planet, third from the sun in a family of nine planets all circling the sun, the star closest to us. We understand our Earth is tiny compared to the size of our star. (I remember being taught as a child that the size of Earth compared to the size of the sun was as a pea relative to a basketball.) The sun is 740 times more massive than the nine major planets together.

The sun is tiny compared to the size of the solar system, the solar system to the size of the Milky Way galaxy, the Milky Way to the size of the Andromeda galaxy, which is twice as big, containing 40 billion stars. And yet the Andromeda galaxy is tiny compared to the universe, which contains billions of other galaxies. All of that, up there, going on at this moment.

This, very sketchily, is the way I perceive the structure of our location within the universe, where we place ourselves in the organization of the celestial objects we recognize around us. On the surface of the earth, we visualize and state our location conventionally by imaginary coordinates, latitude and longitude, by North Pole and South Pole, by hemisphere, by relation to the ocean upon which we sail or beside which we live or the mountain range to the east or to the west, by the geographical and political boundaries of our community. If we say "Montana," most of us can visualize the shape and place of that entity on the globe (North Pole at the top), the same with Puget Sound or the Mississippi River or the Panama Canal.

We visualize the shape of Earth and its continents by the maps and photographs we've been shown, some taken from space, geographical maps, geological maps, computer-generated three-dimensional maps, heat-generated maps recorded by satellite. If you imagine at this moment where you are on the globe in Sitka, something visual must occur. This picture comes to us through science and technology.

We believe, so our story goes, that we are being carried on this spinning Earth that turns on its own axis at a speed so fast we can't even feel it. Our Earth, bearing with it one orbiting moon, meanwhile circles and tilts around the sun, which is itself borne along with the solar system on its path around the center of the Milky Way, the Milky Way and its billions of sun/stars moving as one body—where? Simply away from all other cosmic bodies, a result of the Big Bang theory of the origin of the universe as we currently understand it. We aren't really sitting still at all, but are caught up in this mayhem of motion.

We perceive the time span of our existence, even as a species, as fleeting compared to the life span of some now extinct species (dinosaurs, for example), and we have figures to prove this aspect of our insignificance. Our lives are fleeting compared to the age of the earth, the history of the sun, the solar system, the Milky Way, a pulsar, a quasar. . . .

The story our cosmology tells is that we exist in a universe of flux, not only the rushing river that can never be stepped in twice, but also stars in the process of being born and dying, our own sun in decline, expending itself. (Could anyone come across an article entitled "The

Death of the Sun," as I did recently, and not feel a sudden fear and still-ness in the heart?) We know that the mountains, which once seemed so sure and enduring to other generations in their cosmologies, also have risen and will wear away. Floors of the ocean and platforms under the continents shift and slowly collide, greatly altering the sur-face of the earth. Forests grow up and fall away. Oceans enlarge and decline. Ice sheets form, descend, and retreat. Volcanoes, like Krakatoa, erupt, alter the climate, and affect life on Earth for centu-ries. Strong, successful species gain ascendancy on the earth, eventu-ally wane and vanish. Civilizations full of vibrant and brilliant minds come and go. Our own bodies, the cells of our brains, finely balanced, die and replace themselves constantly.

We also understand our physical being as the result of very slow, apparently random changes, mutations occurring with the DNA, the hereditary code, gradual transformations and adaptations that took place over a very long period of time. We can witness adaptive evo-lutionary changes in some animals (insects, small fish, some birds and amphibians) during our own lifetimes. We have watched our own civilization change and alter the earth, eradicate certain diseases, cre-ate bacterias, manipulate the development of domesticated animals, affect the environment.

Flux and change are constant, so the story goes.

If human consciousness should play a role in the well-being of the universe, we aren't certain what that role is. Our cosmology seems not to address this issue directly. If there is a power or a creator interested in us (though I think the doubt many of us feel in this regard is so deep and pervasive that the issue is hardly mentioned anymore, at least not in the same breath as our cosmology), we aren't certain in what way that power might manifest itself or what vocabulary is suit-able for addressing its existence.

As a result of this cosmology, all of us, I would venture to say, have seen ourselves at some moment or other as "mankind cast aimlessly adrift in a meaningless universe."

To further complicate the story, we have experienced in this cen-tury a sudden and continual influx into our culture of massive amounts of information, information that affects the story our cosmology tells, new information published constantly concerning the heavens and the evolutionary processes of stars, the discovery of new elementary particles, information redefining time, detailed and profuse information on the processes by which animal and plant species function and survive, information about the geological history of the earth and extinct species, information about other human cultures past and present, about the human body, the human brain, the human psyche, information about new technologies that radically alter forms of communication, vigorous exploration of both the very large and the microscopic, even invisible neutrinos, books and books on just the history of the violin, for instance, the history of bread, the history of locks and keys—the history of paperweights, for heaven's sake. You name it and at least one person has written a book about it, with many more, we are certain, to come.

I chose at random one page from the *Oxford-Duden Pictorial English Dictionary*, a dictionary that lists some 28,000 objects from a whole range of technical activities and everyday situations. Listed on this one page are 103 terms dealing simply with roofs and roofing.

I don't believe any previous culture has ever had such a massive vocabulary available to it as does ours today. Every word, *every* word, I believe, a possible metaphor.

All of these oceans of information can be daunting enough, but add to that the fact that much of this information is changing and refining itself continually—and the result is often despair. One is almost fearful to utter a declarative sentence unless its implications are so narrow and qualified—say, for example, "This is how I myself personally think I myself alone might possibly have felt just a moment ago maybe"—that it becomes inane.

So, like the universe, we conceive of our cosmology as constantly changing, altering itself, too, according to new data, more refined methods of gathering information. We are reluctant, then to put our wholehearted faith in all the details of this story, the cosmology as it is constructed today.

This is a very strange and unique facet of our cosmology, that it instructs us not to allow ourselves to fully believe it as it is told today. We must always reserve the right to critically review the cosmology.

The cosmology itself tells us this. This is one of its own characteristics, part of its very own tenets and story—its request for suspension of full commitment, its own insistence on a critical eye and mind at work on itself.

This is very different from the cosmologies of past cultures. Our cosmology tells us we must be willing to accept new, corroborated information that may dismiss or alter parts of its story as previously related. The story adjusts and expands. Rigidity is definitely not a part of our cosmology. Science is not rigid. Dogmas are rigid.

So maybe we like this cosmology, the excitement and astonishment of its grand ideas, the vastness and power and mystery of the universe it describes, the beauty of its intricacies, the freedom of thought it affords. Maybe we love the very fact of its openness, its willingness to adapt itself, its willingness to actually respond to us. That is pretty fine and wonderful, I think.

Or maybe we don't like this cosmology. We might be willing and eager to subscribe to seeing a universe in a grain of sand, but a *changing* universe in *every* grain of sand? At every moment? Our cosmology seems at times to describe a universe that takes no cognizance of us, to describe a universe indifferent to us, "a world of quantity, of reified geometry, a world in which, though there is a place for everything, there is no place for man." Maybe this is the source of much of the literature of despair, or a literature seeking consolation, the literature of seeking consolation in the natural world on Earth. Maybe.

And if we had been given a choice, perhaps we would have created a different cosmology. I'm not arguing that this cosmology is right or wrong, complete or incomplete, eternal or ephemeral, satisfying or disturbing. But I am saying this cosmology is one that is ours. Not only does it provide much of the vocabulary and many of the images of our time, but the way we live and survive physically depends on it. It is integral to our daily lives.

Simply walking out into a wilderness and leaving behind temporarily the life and the accoutrements of our human communities doesn't mean we leave behind this cosmology. It's part of our being. We carry it with us right out onto the tundra, into the rain forest, diving beneath the ocean. In fact, we understand these very designations—*tundra, rain forest, ocean*—in part by the light of our cosmology. The effect of the vision created by our cosmology is evident in Dick Nelson's description of the experience of surfing in Alaska, in his book *The Island Within*:

> Shortly, an even larger series of swells approaches, but I'm far enough out to catch the biggest one and prudent enough to make it my last. As I wade ashore, I watch the energy of the wave die, rushing to the top of the beach and slipping back down again. And I remember its power rising to a crescendo around and under me during the final moments of its life, after traversing a thousand miles of ocean from its birthplace in a far Pacific storm. The motion that so exalted me was given freely by the wave, as the wave was given motion by the wind, as the wind was given motion by the storm, as the storm was given motion by the whirl of the atmosphere and the turning of the earth itself. Then I remember the sea lions, cradled by the same ocean and pleasured by the same waves. All of us here, partaking of a single motion. Together and alive.

And again, Barry Lopez, in "Offshore: A Journey to the Weddell Sea," eloquently describes this vision onboard the *Nathaniel B. Palmer*, an ice-breaking scientific research vessel, as it heads for the southern seas:

> The bridge, its wings cantilevered over ship and ocean on either side and its vast ability to communicate and to navigate in its mute antennas, nearly fills one's field of vision. Above it and beyond tonight is the blackest blue sky riven cleanly by the familiar tingling spine of suns, the Galaxy seen edge-on. Watching the bridge move under the stars, feeling the ship's engines thrum in my legs, and standing in a breeze high above the ocean's smooth, dark plain—and then sensing the plunging depth, the shadowed plain of the Peru Basin below, the complex signal codes of the bioluminescence winking there above the basin floor like stars—I thought, this must be sailing.

This vision of place and relationships, this cosmology, is our myth. We carry it with us in our memories, in our gestures, our bones, just as we carry *Hamlet* or the music of Bach or the Christmas story or the vision of our bedroom at home or the act of turning a page in a book or the face of our mother. There's no getting rid of it. No hope of that.

So what do the underlying concepts of this cosmology that we carry with us do to language? We know our language has been greatly enhanced and enlarged through the vocabulary given us by the sciences. We know that much. How do the images presented us through this cosmology, the vision of planets moving in their orbits through space, the solar system intersected by comets and asteroids, for example, affect the frameworks and metaphors upon which we construct our literature? How does the cosmology affect our choices of subject matter, the tone, confident or abject, in the first line of the poem or essay, our stance toward the hour of the day, the way we regard a rookery of sea lions, eagles clasping claws in midair, the arrow-straight morning sun through the window, across the sheets?

I've already suggested that this cosmology may be the source of much of today's literature of despair, or literature that turns inward, becomes solipsistic, literature seeking consolation in some kind of certainty that is perceived as being absent from our cosmology. But are there effects much more subtle?

And even more crucial, how does our cosmology influence our definitions of loyalty, honesty, dignity, art, love?

We can be sure the effects are there, and in order to develop the strongest beliefs possible—beliefs that enable us to act with conviction, dignity, and generosity—we must understand, recognize, and acknowledge the story of our cosmology, which is shaping the attitudes we take toward ourselves and our world, and also our conceptions of our potentialities. We must learn how to grasp our cosmology fully and to infuse it with a sustaining spirituality.

A statement by Bertrand Russell in *A Free Man's Worship* succinctly defines the despair that can rise from our cosmology:

> That man is the product of causes which had no prevision of the end they were achieving; that his origin, his growth, his hopes and fears, his loves and his beliefs, are but the outcome of accidental collocations of atoms; that no fire, no heroism, no intensity of thought or feeling, can preserve a life beyond the grave; that all the labors of the ages, all

the devotion, all the inspirations, all the noonday brightness of human genius, are destined to extinction in the vast death of the solar system; and the whole temple of Man's achievement must inevitably be buried beneath the debris of a universe in ruins—all these things, if not quite beyond dispute, are yet so nearly certain, that no philosophy which rejects them can hope to stand. Only within the scaffolding of these truths, only on the firm foundation of unyielding despair, can the soul's habitation be safely built.

The point of departure must be "unyielding despair." We start from the recognition of that point to build the soul's habitation.

Beginning there, we should understand that science is in the business of measuring things. Science constructs a model of the universe only from those things that it is able to measure. The model of the universe, the cosmology that science creates, is based on what science is able to measure. It is the fallacy of misplaced concreteness, then, to proclaim that this model is the total reality. The model is not untrue, but only partial, not all-inclusive. If this model were complete, and scientists believed it to be complete, the business of science would come to an abrupt halt. Total truth has not yet been discovered.

Jacob Bronowski, in his book *The Origins of Knowledge and Imagination*, describes another limitation of any investigation of the universe:

I believe that the world is totally connected: this is to say, that there are no events anywhere in the universe which are not tied to every other event in the universe. I regard this to some extent as a metaphysical statement, although you will see, as I develop it in the next lecture, it has a much more down-to-earth content than that. But I will repeat it: I believe that every event in the world is connected to every other event. But you cannot carry on science on the supposition that you are going to be able to connect every event with every other event. . . . It is, therefore, an essential part of the methodology of science to divide the world for any experiment into what we regard as relevant and what we regard, for purposes of that experiment, as irrelevant.

We make a cut. We put the experiment, if you like, into a box. Now the moment we do that, we do violence to the connections in the world. We may have the best cause in the world. I may say, "Well, come on, I am not really going to think that the light from Sirius is going to affect the reading of this micrometer!" And I say this although I can see Sirius clear with the naked eye, and I have the impertinence to say that though the light of Sirius affects my rods and cones it is not going to affect the experiment. Therefore we have always, if I may use another Talmudic phrase, to put a fence round the law, to put a fence round the law of nature that we are trying to tease out. And we have to say, "For purposes of this experiment everything outside here is regarded as irrelevant, and everything inside here is regarded as relevant."

Any effort to investigate the universe, whether through science or literature, involves making a cut in the universe, interrupting its wholeness and unity, and therefore disrupting and ignoring the interconnectedness of all things. Any investigation, poem, or laboratory experiment involves saying "certain things are relevant to this investigation and certain things are not," and once this necessary cut has been made, we have eliminated any possibility of seeing nature and the universe as a whole, in its entirety.

And from Bronowski later in the same book:

The act of imagination is the opening of the system so that it shows new connections. I originally put this idea in *Science and Human Values* when I said that every act of imagination is the discovery of likenesses between two things which were thought unlike. And the example that I gave was Newton's thinking of the likeness between the thrown apple and the moon sailing majestically in the sky. A most improbable likeness, but one which turned out to be (if you will forgive the phrase) enormously fruitful. All acts of imagination are of that kind. They take the closed system, they inspect it, they manipulate it, and then they find something which had not been put into the system so far. They open the system up, they introduce new likenesses, whether it is Shakespeare saying, "My Mistress' eyes are nothing like the Sunne" or it is Newton saying that the moon in essence is exactly like a thrown apple. All those who imagine take parts of the universe which have not been connected hitherto and enlarge the total connectivity of the universe by showing them to be connected.

The creative person, whether scientist or artist, according to Bronowski, is that person who imagines new, different connections, broadening our conception of the universe and its interconnectedness as a whole.

The complete creation of our cosmology, then, must definitely include the model given us by science, this constantly changing and growing model as science itself imagines and discovers new connections. We cannot turn aside from that. But the scientific model must be further enhanced and infused by other human talents and genius, making other new connections. The path to follow, it seems to me, is not contradicting or fighting or turning from science and its beautiful, invigorating story, but assimilating it, incorporating its glory, celebrating both its findings and its method of scrutiny and openness, using its great power and stimulation and beauty as a jumping-off point to an energetic and meaningful spirituality. We are definitely and positively capable of finding and creating spirituality in this cosmology. We have the power and the ability and, possibly, the obligation to do that. We must possess our cosmology rather than being possessed *by* it.

We can begin to do this by making those new imaginative connections and also by examining imaginatively the questions we ask about nature and the universe.

Werner Heisenberg, in *Physics and Philosophy*, states that "natural science does not simply describe and explain nature; it is part of the interplay between nature and ourselves; it describes nature as exposed to our method of questioning."

C. S. Lewis echoes Heisenberg's thought in *The Discarded Image*: "Nature gives most of her evidence in answer to the questions we ask her."

What are the new and startling connections, the innovative questions we may ask of the sycamore leaf, of the wave against the beach, of the raven's call, of the play of a dandelion seed against the sky, of the hands of the lover, of our own involvement in the universe through our observation and delight in these phenomena? We must formulate new questions, ones that will definitely take into account and acknowledge those questions already asked. We must ask questions that accept and incorporate nature's revelations in response to the questions that science asks, but that utilize other realms of investigation, questions that make new connections, new metaphors.

If divinity should rise not from the natural world alone but from our interaction with the natural world, including our interactions with each other, if divinity is created through our manner of bestowing, our reverence, our praise and honor, the gifts we give, and if divinity comes into being likewise through our openness and willingness to receive, then we must ask the questions that allow and encourage these qualities to rise and manifest themselves.

And here's a miracle that must be constantly celebrated: In spite of those moments of the soul's desperation, we do proceed. We do proceed, even in the face of "unyielding despair" that seems sometimes to be the result of the truths listed by Bertrand Russell. We do continue to attempt to build the soul's habitation. And we do it partially by expressing the awe and thrill and gratitude we feel at the mystery and beauty of the universe as it continues to reveal itself to us through all human disciplines. Being one ourselves with the universe, we continue to create it, to infuse it with meaning, as it continues to reveal and inform us, body and soul. We embrace strongly, as we are in turn embraced by the stars, the heavens, the earth, embraced by the universe through our very revelry in it.

WORKS CITED

Bronowski, Jacob. *The Origins of Knowledge and Imagination*. New Haven: Yale University Press, 1978.

Harrison, Edward R. *Cosmology: The Science of the Universe*. Cambridge: Cambridge University Press, 1981.

Heisenberg, Werner. *Physics and Philosophy*. New York: Harper and Row, 1958.

Koyre, A. *Newtonian Studies*. London: Chapman and Hall, 1965.

Lewis, C. S. *The Discarded Image*. Cambridge: Cambridge University Press, 1967.

Lopez, Barry. "Offshore: A Journey to the Weddell Sea." *Orion*. Winter 1994.

Nelson, Richard. *The Island Within*. San Francisco: North Point Press, 1989.

Russell, Bertrand. *A Free Man's Worship*. Portland, Maine: Mosher, 1923.

Knowers and Makers

Describing the Universe

In being immeasurably fewer, the worlds of that day will be immeasurably greater than our own. Then, indeed, amid unfathomable abysses, will be glaring, unimaginable suns. . . . While undergoing consolidation, the clusters themselves, with a speed prodigiously accumulative, have been rushing towards their own general centre—and now, with a thousand-fold electric velocity, commensurate only with their material grandeur and with the spiritual appetite for oneness, the majestic remnants of the tribe of Stars flash, at length, into a common embrace.—Edgar Allan Poe, *Eureka*, 1848

One hypothesis that accounts for many recent radio and X-ray observations of Centaurus A is the following: The engine that generates the radio plasma has at its center a black hole with the mass of a billion suns. The black hole is surrounded by a toroidal accretion disk made up of gas and dust. Fuel for the engine comes from infalling gas, which could be tidally torn from the atmosphere of stars near the disk.—*Scientific American*, 1983

For his final work, *Eureka*, Edgar Allan Poe claimed the genre of poetry. While it contains one of Poe's humorous hoaxes, the bulk of the prose piece is a descriptive cosmology. Remarkably, Poe modulates between the language of scientific treatise and transcendental philosophy, lucidly drawing from the Western scientific observations of Herschel, Laplace, Mädler, and others, as well as the *Bhagavad Gita*. As the epigraphs show, there remain many resonances between Poe's mid-nineteenth-century poem and some of today's most probable cosmological models as discussed in Stephen Hawking's *A Brief History of Time*. Poe proposes an initial expansion of the universe, invisible massive stars, and a final collapse where "the stellar bodies would finally be merged into one," the scattered Godhead finally reassembled, where matter will be "Matter without matter . . . Matter no more." Hawking speaks of cosmology similarly, but in the current scientific idiom of Big Bangs, Black Holes, and the Big Crunch. In modern physics the universe and its dark matter will fall into the abyss of a final singularity; in this massive singularity, the laws of physics that differentiate between matter and energy, in real time at least, will break down. Hawking's argument, too, is laced with discussions of the relationship between scientific theory and metaphysical inquiry, though he holds spiritualism at a scientifically appropriate distance. Intermediately, and perhaps unsurprisingly, Paul Valéry's assessment of Poe's cosmogony ought then to apply to much current theory and to the claims of both writers:

> The author seems to have been a precursor of those bold spirits who would rescue the universe from a certain death by means of an infinitely brief passage through an infinitely improbable state.

Poetry and science should say much to each other. As children, we begin as both scientists and poets, knowers and makers. Yet the past three or four centuries suggest that the relationship between knowing and making has been at best uneasy, and occasionally confrontational (especially when institutional funding is at issue.) From most literary points of view, poetry would raise us to an irrational heaven at the same time science would turn us into decadent descendants of apes.[1] Yet literature and science, despite the appearance of separation, have always maintained an interest in each other. After science and literature were unyoked from the medieval Church that for ages superimposed its motives on all disciplines, each was forced to redefine its objectives in an increasingly secular world. Concomitantly, each discipline had to renegotiate its relationship with and against the other, so it should not be surprising that evidence of the science-literature dialogue shows up in both fields.

In literature over the past several centuries, science is unavoidable: *Paradise Lost* is luminous with astronomical observations; *Tristram Shandy* humorously parodies the sciences of obstetrics, fortification, and a kind of mechanistic "hobbyhorse" psychology; Wordsworth's *Prelude* and its River Derwent certainly studies narrative as chaotic turbulence (even Coleridge complains of his propensity to "eddy"); cetologists marvel at the scope of Melville's *Moby Dick*, which is certainly a cosmology; George Eliot opens *Daniel Deronda* by naming poetry as science's "absent-minded grandmother," and, as Gillian Beer points out, she has structured her novel on James Clerk Maxwell's theory of the ring atom.

In the twentieth century, science's influence on literature grew exponentially. Conrad's *The Secret Agent*, published in 1906 and also structured with Maxwell's ring atom in mind, is a kind of thermodynamic allegory with an eye on "social physics" or applied probabilistics in the entropic late nineteenth century. Joyce and Beckett frequently employ and parody the language of scientific inquiry in their works. Marianne Moore, William Carlos Williams, and, in an oblique way, Wallace Stevens were all trained as scientists, and their poems frequently arise out of questions of observation, scientific questions. Randall Jarrell maintained that Robert Frost's sonnet "Design" was about quantum mechanics. Thomas Pynchon's *Gravity's Rainbow* synthesized the relevance of science to literature, to all humanity, with all of its promise and threat, pleasure and paranoia. And of course, we haven't even mentioned science fiction, the overarching influence of Darwinism and psychology, or Kathy Acker, Donna Haraway, William Gibson, and (can we call it this?) the cyberpunk tradition.

Of course, science hasn't ignored literature. Epiphany, in fact, is more frequently a scientific term, as we can see from the myth, if not the fact, of Newton's apple. And Newton's rival in the optical sciences, Goethe, gave us a Faust for the ages. More recently, Friedrich August Kekulé dreamed the Ourobouros into a benzene serpent. James Clerk

Maxwell's articulation of the second law of thermodynamics relied on an intuition and an analogic leap, drawing from sociology and the law of probabilities (molecules were like people?). In fact, Maxwell's theory of gases began the reinstallation of uncertainty into the realm of objective science, eroding the smug primacy of positivist determinism. Maxwell also published poetry, including poems like "The Vampyre." The literariness of Darwin's *Origin of the Species* made his book a best-seller in his day, and his work remains, along with Freud's, one of the most studied scientific texts in the last hundred years. This century, Einstein created a relative universe, then balked for spiritual reasons at the uncertainties Heisenberg and Bohr ultimately made of it. What would we call the fundamental building blocks of matter, if Murray Gell-Mann hadn't remembered the phrase "three quarks for Muster Mark" from *Finnegan's Wake*? Well, now there are six quarks, and they bear the names up, down, top, bottom, strange, and charm, end words to some quantum sestina. Modern cosmologies posit an infinite number of possible universes, all existing, so that, somewhere, sometime, we take the road not taken, and all the lies we ever make up are true, inevitable. There are so many realisms. And most recently, as we move forward in science and mathematics, we seem to move backward into our oldest mythologies, into the fractal depths of chaos theory. And our skies continue to fill with our myths, because astronomers from all ages have looked to our stories to name the stars.

On an Etruscan vase in the Louvre figures of children are seen blowing bubbles. Those children probably enjoyed their occupation just as modern children do. Our admiration of the beautiful and delicate forms, growing and developing themselves, the feeling that it is our breath which is turning dirty soapsuds into spheres of splendour, the fear lest by any irreverent touch we may cause the gorgeous vision to vanish with a sputter of soapy water in our eyes, our wistful gaze as we watch the perfected bubble when it sails from the pipe's mouth to join, somewhere in the sky, all the other beautiful things that have vanished before it, assure us that, whatever our nominal age may be, we are of the same family as those Etruscan children.

Here, for instance, we have a book, in two volumes, written by a distinguished man of science, and occupied for the most part with the theory and practice of bubble-blowing. Can the poetry of bubbles survive this? Will not the lovely visions which have floated before the eyes of untold generations collapse at the rude touch of Science, and "yield their place to cold material laws"? No, we need go no further than this book and its author to learn that the beauty and mystery of natural phenomena may make such an impression on a fresh and open mind that no physical obstacle can ever check the course of thought and study which it has once called forth.—James Clerk Maxwell, "Plateau on Soap-Bubbles," *Nature* 10 (1874)

Poets and critics who would derogate the influence of science on contemporary verse might turn to Walt Whitman's "When I Heard the Learn'd Astronomer" for support. He walks out "tired and sick" of a lecture on astronomy to "look up in perfect silence at the stars." Yet we do not ask what drew Whitman to the lecture in the first place, or whether astronomers should not walk out of boring poetry readings. The answer is obvious. Just by showing up, Whitman suggests the kind of intellectual balance that a good scientist would appreciate, a balance Maxwell certainly exhibits in the above beautifully composed review. So, poets should go to astronomy lectures, interrogate the scientific worldview, study fractal geometry and chaos theory, or even analyze garbage, as A. R. Ammons does so masterfully in *Garbage*. What better for our poetry than to have a scientist around, even an internal one, to point out how unaccountably wrong or irrational our poetic perceptions can sometimes be, our worst analogies, our occasional propensities to alchemy because we can't see a truer beauty in the periodic table of the elements? Many poets writing today— Ammons, Christopher Buckley, Albert Goldbarth, and Pattiann Rogers, to name a few of the finest—could just as well give as attend lay lectures on science. And while they might take a break from a colloquium on quantum fluctuation, go out, smoke a little, or speak to a friend and look up at the stars that don't go away no matter how much we talk about them, these poets always go back in. They understand the liminal nature of their task and the unsettling translations poets must make between subjectivity and objectivity and back. They must inhabit a multitude of worlds, of spaces and times, to recover a semblance of nature, of home, of self and other, of the grand "project" of being alive and conscious in the universe.

The previous sentence also describes the efforts of our most brilliant scientists today as John Horgan presents them in his occasionally dismissive assessment of the future of science. In *The End of Science* (1996), Horgan never addresses poetry per se, nor poetry's influence on science over the centuries. Rather, Horgan maintains that science has discovered almost all of the major ideas that it can reasonably expect to test empirically about the universe. Thus, in Horgan's view, the science practiced by such visionaries as Noam Chomsky, Murray Gell-Mann, Stephen Jay Gould, Stephen Hawking, Marvin Minsky, Ilya Prigogine, John Wheeler, and Edward Witten is more akin to literature than the science of the last hundred and fifty years. For Horgan, modern science is "ironic," and merely theorizes in a realm of "negative capability" insofar as superstring theory, complexity, quantum chromodynamics, artificial intelligence, and other theories pose seemingly unsolvable or unprovable problems for modern science and the society that must pay for it. But the true irony is that Horgan is merely being rhetorical. By ending science, as it were, he can feel free to posit his own theocosmogony based upon a personal "mystical" experience, a theocosmogony that suggests that our universe exists because God is afraid of being lonely and flees His or Her own solipsism expansively and according to the Hubble constant. What it boils down to, though, is that Horgan wants to tell his own story about the universe—one that comes from the heart, from something he witnessed and wants to witness, where all stories come from, after all.

Horgan is not the first science commentator to write about the end of science and its metaphysical implications. Ernst Haeckel, the most famous embryologist of his day, wrote of the same issues in *The Riddle of the Universe at the Close of the Nineteenth Century*.[2] Frequently quoting Goethe, Haeckel finally argued for a monistic, mechanistic philosophy that excluded all concepts of deity except, reluctantly, pantheism. The only reason he allowed for any concept of deity in the universe stemmed from the "final" unsolved riddle, the riddle of substance, the how of matter. Yet scientists continue to pursue this elusive goal and continue to find new depths to matter, new questions to ask. Henry Adams, in his fascinating but little regarded *The Tendency of History*, discusses the relationship of entropy to history in direct opposition to Haeckel's evolutionary viewpoint, and he cites mathematician Lucien Poincaré to support his viewpoint that all we can strive to become in this universe of ideas, this "multiverse," are

"Chief Anarchists."[3] Adams thus repudiates any deterministic principle of supervening law that might reduce the universe to a simple mechanism, and most "Romantic" scientists Horgan interviews would agree.

In a sense, though, Horgan is right about science, but I would phrase it less dubiously and say instead that science is rediscovering its Romantic roots. Every search for the truth begins as a crazy dream, with a small lamp and a lot of steps. Despite its empirical methodologies, science fundamentally seeks truth, so there is no reason to deny its Romantic element. Poe in his poem *Eureka* felt no need to jettison science to describe an ironic, fragmented God in his theocosmogony. So Horgan's predictions of the end of science, like Haeckel's, are inevitably premature. Science will never end, except through a failure of the imagination or a false or "fanciful" idealization of it. What this means for each scientist is that the task is to keep looking, just as the task for the poet is to keep making. Imagine poets assuming that Homer, after laying down the rules, had said all there was to say about the epic. We would today be without the incredible achievements of Dante, Spenser, Milton, Wordsworth, Melville, or even James Merrill and Thomas Pynchon. And I sincerely doubt that any of the scientists Horgan interviews intend to stop formulating new theories about how the universe works.

Each way of seeing contributes to the total human endeavor; each description of the universe adds to our ability to see further into the depths of the universe, or into the depths of our own consciousness. Poets and scientists alike desire to describe and create, to tell stories about the universe and to clear a space for new ideas, new ways of thinking. And whether we tell our stories in verse or in Maxwell's field equations, it is our mutual ability to describe the universe that ultimately brings our endeavors together. It should not surprise us that many of the poets writing today find inspiration, not only in the stars, but in the fuzzy and beautiful blobs they make in the higher wavelengths that only the Hubble telescope can help us discern. And if science is moving into a phase of negative capability, a state I argue science cannot abandon if it is to thrive, then the Grand Unified Theory, or the theory of everything, is where we begin, not where we'll end. All human endeavors to know, physics and metaphysics alike, began under the aegis of philosophy. While we have overspecialized in order to define finer and finer distinctions among fields of knowledge, it becomes increasingly apparent that the further one goes into a field, the more one discovers its relationship to all the others. To deny this interrelationship is to attempt to maintain a level of blindness, to keep fields of knowledge political and competitive despite their commonalities. So if we move through any "specialty" with our eyes open, we eventually go back toward philosophy, toward the simple love of knowledge that all fields of learning are founded upon.

Keats, who gave us the term "negative capability," also outlined the most useful "theory of everything" in his poem "Ode on a Grecian Urn" when he concludes:

> "Beauty is Truth, truth beauty,"—that is all
> Ye know on earth, and all ye need to know.

And of course, if one reads poetry or listens to scientists engaged in theoretical discussions, what Keats says "is all" for poets and scientists alike. And just as no one can deny the elegance of Keats's odes, no one can deny the aesthetic attractiveness of Andre Linde's fractal self-reproducing inflationary universe. It is beautiful, and it explains some things. It won't be the last theory, but Keats will not have written the last ode either. And perhaps Paul Valéry again brings this issue to the most cogent close, the most useful and oldest conflation of science and poetry, when he observes that "cosmogony is one of the oldest of all literary forms."

NOTES

1. Most notably, Ilse Bulhof, George Levine, N. Katherine Hayles, Gillian Beer, and a few others are beginning to study and challenge the language of modern science and its rhetorical claims to objectivity, despite the deception of its passive voice and argument through consensus. For example, Ilse Bulhof (*The Language of Science* [Leiden: E. J. Brill, 1992]) traces the commonly accepted rift between science and literature to Renaissance and Baroque developments in the arts, sciences, and philosophical inquiry. To grossly oversimplify, a poetical-rhetorical understanding of the interpret-

able "book of nature" was undermined by advancements in technology, such as Galileo's development of the telescope, the development of mathematical laws like Boyle's Law, and by the invention of the printing press, which instituted the primacy of the printed text over the spoken word. In short, science's increasing nominalism silenced nature, which "lost her capacity to witness" (141). Instead, the language of nature became quantifiable, mechanistic, mathematical, and therefore (until the advent of modern physics) utterly deterministic, utterly unpoetic. Bulhof finally argues that the resurgence of a hermeneutical ontology successfully questions science's objectivity, its separateness from nature, and proposes that science must morally reject its claims of observing immediate truths. Here I endeavor to suggest that literature and science remained in dialogue throughout this period despite the superficial appearance of separation.

2. Haeckel originated the idea that "ontogeny recapitulates phylogeny," that the development of the embryo passes through phases that parallel the development of more and more sophisticated phyla (e.g., mammals) over time. Thus, theoretically, the human embryo passes through invertebrate to fish to amphibian phases, etc., on the way to becoming a mammal, and inscribes a kind of palimpsest of Darwinian evolution, as well as evidence that evolution was irrefutable. Haeckel was incorrect, yet the theory has been taught in schools even into the 1970s. Haeckel's views on race and religion are even more problematic, since he followed the eugenicist Sir Francis Galton in supposing Jews to be an inferior race. Haeckel, refuting divine conception, argued that Christ was the illegitimate son of a Roman soldier who engendered Christ with his more "noble" non-Semitic qualities. It should not be surprising that such "scientific" assertions informed the views of the anti-Semitic intelligentsia, including perhaps Ezra Pound and T. S. Eliot.

3. Poincaré, from the same family as the more renowned proto-chaos theorist Henri Poincaré, explains, "A certain anarchy reigns in the sciences of nature's domain; ... any venture may be risked; no law appears rigorously necessary," or deterministic, to update the idiom (104).

WORKS CITED

Adams, Henry. *The Tendency of History*. 1919. Reprint, New York: Macmillan, 1928.

Beer, Gillian. *Darwin's Plots: Evolutionary Narrative in Darwin, George Eliot, and Nineteenth-Century Fiction*. Boston: Routledge & Kegan Paul, 1983.

Bulhof, Ilse. *The Language of Science*. Leiden: E. J. Brill, 1992.

Haeckel, Ernst. *The Riddle of the Universe at the Close of the Nineteenth Century*. Trans. Joseph McCabe. New York: Harper, 1900.

Hawking, Stephen. *A Brief History of Time: From the Big Bang to Black Holes*. New York: Bantam Books, 1988.

Horgan, John. *The End of Science: Facing the Limits of Knowledge in the Twilight of the Scientific Age*. Reading, Mass.: Addison-Wesley, Helix Books, 1996.

Keats, John. *Complete Poems*. Ed. Jack Stillinger. Cambridge: Belknap Press of Harvard University Press, 1982.

Maxwell, James Clerk. "Plateau on Soap-Bubbles." *Nature* 10 (1874).

Poe, Edgar Allan. *Eureka: A Prose Poem*. New York: G. P. Putnam, 1848.

Valéry, Paul. *Leonardo, Poe, Mallarmé*. Vol. 8 of *The Collected Works of Paul Valéry*. Trans. Malcolm Cowley and James R. Lawler. Princeton: Princeton University Press, 1972.

KELLY CHERRY

The Two Cultures at the End
of the Twentieth Century

In his essay "The Two Cultures," first published in the *New Statesman* in 1956 and later included in a series of lectures delivered at Cambridge University, C. P. Snow said of himself, "By training I was a scientist; by vocation I was a writer. . . . It was a piece of luck, if you like, that arose through coming from a poor home." I, too, came from a poor home, though it was an educated home, and my parents, who were string-quartet violinists, thought that economic salvation would lie in having one of their children turn out to be a scientist. I never got further than a hodgepodge of introductory science courses and rather more math, but even that superficial acquaintance with science has proved to be "a piece of luck." I have taken seriously what C. P. Snow called the problem of "the two cultures"—that "the intellectual life of the whole of Western society is increasingly being split into two polar groups"—and have tried to find ways in my writing to reunite what had been separated, to bring together what had been estranged, to fuse, as it were, what had been fissioned. If the results are essentially private, well, that is because those scientists and scholars over there on the other side of the chasm need to get busy and do *their* part, by, of course, reading some contemporary poetry.

C. P. Snow may seem an unfashionable figure by now; he's probably unknown to most younger people. Despite his many novels, none of my writing students has ever heard of him. But there was a time when, in the heat of the Cold War, in the Race to Space, his essay came as a call to arms. In October 1957, Sputnik went up—and C. P. Snow's analysis of "the two cultures" was thought to have been prophetic.

Thus it was that some time later, at the age of seventeen, I found myself a sophomore at the New Mexico Institute of Mining and Technology. My being a student at a mining school, precisely because it *was* such a ridiculous thing for me to be, is a good indication of the values the country held at that time. I recall sitting in a classroom with mining students and young engineers, budding atmospheric physicists and possibly a future oil magnate or two, taking an IQ test for spatial perspective. Thousands of miles from my home in Virginia, wearing East Coast hemlines that were shockingly short in the fifties Southwest, I chewed on my pencil and tried to figure out how many hidden sides a two-dimensional object might possess. I believe I had the lowest IQ ever recorded at New Mexico Tech.

All the same, like loving a man the world has said you may not marry, I lived in a kind of constant scientific swoon, ravished by the beauty of mathematics, the complicated narrative of paleontology, the diagrams of vectors in our physics notebooks, Mondrian in their clarity.

If spatial configurations were not my forte, temporal ones may have been. Even before I read C. P. Snow, I liked almost nothing better, during high school, than to listen to the Beethoven quartets, which are the most beautiful explorations of time ever conducted in music, late at night while drawing up charts of geologic eras and periods at my desk. I had an attic room, with dormer windows. You could listen to music there without disturbing the rest of the house. And so, late at night, the whole house was sound asleep—sleeping sound; sound, sleeping—except for my room, which was wakeful with sublime music and the meditation of time, that long line next to which my own life, at fourteen, was not so much as a visible dot.

Some of the images of those nights that I spent lost in time returned to me as I was working on my book of poetry *Natural Theology*. I chose to open this book with a poem titled "Phylogenesis," and perhaps, as I wrote it, I was remembering the vivid intellectual fantasies of my youth:

She cracks her skin
like a shell, and goes in

She camps in her womb
She sucks the marrow from her bones

and sips bison's blood
in the afternoon; for years,

snow piles outside the cave she burrows in
She wakes to warm weather,

fur on her four feet, grass
rising and falling in waves like water

She feeds on flowering plants,
enjoys a cud of orchid and carrot

In the Middle Permian, scales slippery as shale appear
on her back; her spine unfurls a sail broadside

to the sun, filling with a light like wind, while *Sphenodon*
turns its third eye on the sky, sensing

rain, and rock salt washes into the ocean
Silent as mist, she slides down a mud bank on her underbelly

Lobe-finned and fleshy,
she pumps air through her gills

She's soft as jelly
Her skull is limestone

She drifts, like a continent
or a protozoan, on the planet's surface,

and sinks into the past
like a pebble into a brackish pool

The seas catch fire
The earth splits and gapes

The earth cracks open like an egg
and she goes in

We begin

Whatever else may be said about that poem, I am pretty sure that it is
the only poem ever to get into it a reference to *Sphenodon*, a predecessor of the modern lizard. I hope that this is a scientific enough
reference to appease the spirit of C. P. Snow. After complaining that
"it is bizarre how very little of twentieth-century science has been
assimilated into twentieth-century art," he admitted wryly that, at
least, "now and then one used to find poets conscientiously using
scientific expressions, and getting them wrong—there was a time
when 'refraction' kept cropping up in verse in a mystifying fashion,
and when 'polarised light' was used as though writers were under the
illusion that it was a specially admirable kind of light." And I know
that when black holes began to be talked about in *Time* and *Newsweek*,
they were suddenly cropping up in poems everywhere (mine too), as
if the mere importation of a scientific term into a poem were enough
to freight the poem with new meaning. It isn't, of course.

No, the challenge of using science in poetry lies in using it in a way
that results in stronger poetry, a poetry that incorporates as much as
possible of the real world. One contemporary poet who has been
much drawn to the bleak romance of astronomy as a way of training
a telescope on the real world we live in is Robert Watson. In certain
of his poems we come to know an astronomer's stubborn love for
space itself, as if the distance between two objects were more seduc-
tive than any mere object itself could be. "This is a universe of luck
and chance," Watson writes in "The Radio Astronomer," and continues, "Galaxies / Spin in flight like snow, rattle in space, are gone."

In another poem, "Riding in Space I Kiss My Wife," he allows us to
view a more mundane romance through the lens of the speaker's ro-

mance with the "universe of luck and chance," so that we see our messy, mortal world as if from very far away, from as far away as cosmic unconcern:

> Over us in bed together kissing,
> The night rides,
> Dumps a splintered ice-boat, its shrouds,
> The universe in our bed, our children's beds.
> The arteries of heaven run bursting with cars.
> "There are billions of galaxies," I read,
> "And a galaxy contains countless billions of stars."

Watson's use of astronomical imagery heightens, brilliantly, the sense of despair in his poems; it extends despair, the sense of overwhelming distance between actuality and ideal, into a lyricism of the first magnitude.

The poet and fiction writer R. H. W. Dillard, whose vocabularies of reference are astonishingly varied and knowledgeably detailed, encompassing, among others, science, cinema, literature, art, and linguistics, takes as an epigraph the philosopher of process A. N. Whitehead's pronunciamento, "The stable universe is slipping away from under us," to enter a poem, "March Again," about the fixity of love:

> Christ could have swum away
> From the cross on air,
> But he chose to be nailed
> To the ground. You grow dizzy
> And each step is like walking
> On water. . . .

Reading Whitehead, the writer has recognized in an idea about the world something that can be employed not only as hypothesis or conclusion but as a way of thinking, an approach to *another* idea. This, after all, is central to what writers, I believe, want to do. They don't want just to embellish the world with images, decking the world's hall with bough after bough of holly. They want to lead the reader through the hall into all the rooms that lie beyond. A way to get to those rooms is by using an *idea* as an image.

For instance, in the long poem, "A Bird's-Eye View of Einstein," that closes my collection *Relativity: A Point of View*, I turned to the theory of relativity as a way of thinking about the Trinity, three-in-one, and especially about the Trinity as it might manifest itself—or its selves—to a woman's point of view. There is a phrase, "duets with Einstein," that might seem to the uninitiated to be the whole of my use of the theory of relativity in that poem, but in fact the whole poem is predicated on the theory, presenting, as it does, a series of parallel triads through which the point of view slides in a very strange way, bending the time of the poem back on itself like reflected—or possibly refracted, and maybe even polarized—light.

Still, what the poet wants to make of science is not more science but more poetry. I have to admit that I am not always bothered by an excessive need to be factual (though I hope, always and forever, to be truthful). In a longish narrative poem I tried to imagine a scientific expedition in Siberia in 1913. I have no idea whether an expedition like the one in the poem ever actually took place, and yet an encounter with a prehistoric creature that has been frozen during an Ice Age to reemerge into life thousands of years later certainly recurs again and again as a kind of unarticulated myth, and so I decided to articulate it. I picked the year 1913 out of the historical air, to increase the tension: World War I is about to begin; the Russian Revolution is waiting in the wings. Readers have asked me about the paleobotanist who appears in the poem and is named Szymanowski. There may well be a paleobotanist named Szymanowski, but I have never read of him. The only Szymanowski I know of was a Polish violinist, and I know of him only because, finding myself in need of a name that would provide a satisfying mouthful of syllables in my poem, I raced downstairs—I was visiting my parents at the time—and asked my father what he could suggest. My father, not having read C. P. Snow, seized upon what he knew best and came up with the name "Szymanowski." I believe that if I had just stayed downstairs he could have found me a violinist's name that would do for every occupation I might ever have literary occasion to refer to. I ran with "Szymanowski" back to my room and stuck it into my poem. What is important, sometimes, is the scheme of science rather than the science itself, although I suspect the scheme will not likely occur to writers who don't regularly include science as one of the things they think about. For example, in a poem about the rose, which I wanted to convey in all its traditional romantic, theological, and literary dimensions, I took a botanical lecture as my model for the poem's form. Each description that the poem gives of "the rose" is presented as a definition, as if something scientifically taxonomic were going on, which, of course, it is not:

THE ROSE
A botanical lecture

It's the cup of blood,
the dark drink lovers sip,
the secret food

It's the pulse and elation
of girls on their birthdays,
it's good-byes at the railroad station

It's the murmur of rain,
the blink of daylight
in a still garden, the clink
of crystal; later, the train

pulling out, the white cloth,
apples, pears, and champagne—
good-bye! good-bye!
We'll weep petals, and dry
our tears with thorns

A steep country springs up beyond
the window, with a sky like a pond

a flood. It's a rush
of bright horror, a burning bush,
night's heart,
the living side of the holy rood

It's the whisper of grace in the martyrs' wood

Writing that poem, I felt as though having access to the *idea*, at least, of a botanical lecture gave me a new route into an otherwise familiar place, arguably even an overtrafficked place, in the land of poetic symbolism. It gave me a new take on an old problem. It worries me that so many writing students confine themselves to the study of literature—and literature in English, at that. Obviously, writers need to know their own literatures as well as possible, but that is not all they need to know. I think it is unfortunate for students that so many of them are now able to earn college degrees without taking serious courses in science and math (and let's throw classical literature in there while we are at it). There is a world out there to be written about.

Because, the truth is, I am an empiricist at heart, and I do believe that there is a world out there but that it is a world difficult to know. I believe we must bring every instrument at our disposal to bear on the knowing of it. And science is one of those instruments, but so is literature. Literature is not merely an ornament or a therapy; it is a way of knowing the world. This is what *scientists* need to understand about *literature*.

(I will go even further, all the way out on a theoretical limb, and state that different forms of literature are essentially different modes of perception, though each form partakes to some degree of the others: fiction is the way we come to know the world of relation; the personal essay is the way we come to know—more than the subject of its discussion—the mind of the essayist, how thinking occurs; poetry, for all the use it makes of emotion, is the way we come to know the thing itself, the simple undeniable fact of existence, of existence in all its manifold particularity.)

If it is clear that literature (and other art) is a kind of knowledge, it is equally clear that math and science are forms of beauty, to anyone who will recognize them as such. I will never forget that day in a classroom at the University of Virginia when Ian Hacking was attempting to explain to a group of graduate students Gödel's proof of the impossibility of establishing the presence of internal logical consistency in deductive systems. Some of the students were working on their doctorates in mathematics; others of us were philosophy students dazed by the entire mad enterprise of mathematical logic, and for weeks we had been wondering how we were ever going to get out of this class alive. Hacking went to the blackboard and proceeded to work his way around the room until all four walls were white with chalked equations constituting an abbreviated version of the proof. And suddenly, I went from being dazed to being dazzled, as everything revealed itself to me. It was a vision, surely, not unlike the moment of illumination I experienced when, at five, I finally, after great effort, learned how to tie my shoelaces—but that was a triumph too, a door opening onto a universe of pattern and intricacy and scope. It was like reading Shakespeare or listening to Beethoven. It was beauty, pure and simple, or not so simple, and if I no longer remember anything I ever knew of mathematical logic, I have never forgotten the sheer gorgeousness of it. This is what *writers* need to understand about *mathematics and science.*

Two books of poetry published in the seventies spoke directly to the writer's responsibility to understand what he can of mathematics and science. John Bricuth, in *The Heisenberg Variations*, an extremely interesting and often very funny collection, evokes a contemporary sense of uncertainty, our sense that we are probably, right now, the butt of a joke we don't quite get. Here is "Talking Big":

> We are sitting here at dinner talking big.
> I am between the two dullest men in the world
> Across from the fattest woman I ever met.
> We are talking big. Someone has just remarked
> That energy equals the speed of light squared.
> We nod, feeling that that is "pretty nearly correct."
> I remark that the square on the hypotenuse can more
> Than equal the squares on the two sides. The squares
> On the two sides object. The hypotenuse over the way
> Is gobbling the grits. We are talking big. The door
> Opens suddenly revealing a vista that stretches
> To infinity. Parenthetically, someone remarks
> That a body always displaces its own weight.
> I note at the end of the gallery stands a man
> In a bowler and a black coat with an apple where
> His head should be, with his back to me, and it is me.

I clear my throat and re (parenthetically) mark
That a body always falls of its own weight.
"whoosh-WHOOM!" sighs the hypotenuse across,
And (godknows) she means it with all her heart.

Who are the squares on the two sides, if not ourselves? And we are talking big, but no matter how big, "a body always displaces its own weight." Who is the man in the bowler and black coat? Traditionally Death, he is also, here, the speaker in the poem, who will displace his own weight. Does he always represent the death of the Newtonian universe, those reasonable laws displaced by the apple of relativity? And is the apple also the apple of the knowledge of good and evil? Oh, the poet *meant* it when he said, "We are talking big."

Al Zolynas, in *The New Physics*, takes an opposite tack, turning to the unseen structures of subatomic physics to comment on our daily life in the middle range. His book is divided into three sections, "Color," "Charm," and "Strangeness," as if the most miniscule particles of the world, quarks, were also metaphors for it. In the title poem, a prose poem, he explains his method:

> And so, the closer he looks at things, the farther away they seem. At dinner, after a hard day at the universe, he finds himself slipping through his food. His own hands wave at him from beyond a mountain of peas. Stars and planets dance with molecules on his fingertips. After a hard day with the universe, he tumbles through himself, flies through the dream galaxies of his own heart. In the very presence of his family he feels he is descending through an infinite series of Chinese boxes.
>
> This morning, when he entered the little broom-closet of the electron looking for quarks and neutrinos, it opened into an immense hall, the hall into a plain—the Steppes of Mother Russia! He could see men hauling barges up the river, chanting faintly for their daily bread.
>
> It's not that he longs for the old Newtonian Days, although something of plain matter and simple gravity might be reassuring, something of the good old equal-but-opposite forces. And it's not that he hasn't learned to balance comfortably on the see-saw of paradox. It's what he sees in the eyes of his children—the infinite black holes, the ransomed light at the center.

What we want to know, what we crave to know, is, of course, the answer to the oldest questions: Why are we—even our children—made to die? Why must the good suffer? Can we be good? Why should we be good? Is there point of purpose to our existence? These are the questions both scientists and poets would like to know the answers to. If none has yet fathomed a single answer, we may acknowledge that the questions themselves compose a kind of Rosetta stone. Asking the same questions in our different languages of science and art, we learn to translate ourselves into one another, we see that we are different words for the same humanity. There is a vision of oneness here, amid the many voices in which the universe speaks its own being. In "The Study of Ecology," Dillard says that Thoreau, examining the veins of leaves against sunlight,

> Also looked at his hand—
> Branching, veined, barked,
> The fine black hairs
> That need sunlight to be seen,
> Lines, branches, the universal M,
> Cain's mark.
>
> Raise your hand, hold it,
> Know the stilling of winter,
> And when you grow tired, forget
> And let it fall, the flow
> Of new springs.
>
> You rub your eyes,
> Bone, skin on water,
> You see heavens, stars,
> Fires, fire.
>
> Leaves riddle with sunlight
> The ground, the grass,
> Your hand, holding sunlight,
> Leaves of shadow, of air.

This is to say that both kinds of knowing, literature and science, are vehicles that carry us out of our solipsistic selves and into the world. Both make it possible for us to recognize one another as real beings moving in a real world. I tried to say something like this in a poem in which I imagined the world as it might have been viewed by the first woman to orbit the earth, in 1963, Lt. Col. Valentina Vladimirovna Tereshkova. The poem itself makes an orbit, closing in a circle, and pulls lines from Genesis and Job into its scientific compass. (I should mention that the Daugava is a river in Latvia, one of the Baltic countries whose rightfully independent status has now been recognized. That the Daugava, in this poem, is "tangy" is an allusion to—what else?—Tang, fabled orange drink of space missions!)

It looked like an apple
or a Christmas orange:
I wanted to eat it.
I could taste the juice
trickling down my throat,
my tongue smarted,
my teeth were chilled.
How sweet those mountains seemed,
how cool and tangy, the Daugava!

What scrawl of history
had sent me so far from home? . . .

When I was a girl in school, comrades,
seemingly lazy as a lizard
sprawled on a rock in Tashkent,
I dreamed of conquest.

My hands tugged at my arms,
I caught flies on my tongue.

Now my soul's as hushed as the Steppes on a winter night;
snow drifts in my brain, something
shifts, sinks, subsides inside,

and some undying pulse hoists my body
like a flag, and sends me up,
like Nureyev.
From my samovar I fill my cup with air,
and it overflows.
Who knows who scatters the bright cloud?

Two days and almost twenty-three hours
I looked at light,
scanning its lines like a book.

My conclusions:

At last I saw the way
time turns,
like a key in a lock,
and night becomes day,
and sun burns away the primeval mist,
and day is, and is not.

Listen, earthmen,
comrades of the soil,
I saw the Black Sea shrink to a drop
of dew and disappear;
I could blot out Mother Russia with my thumb in thin air;
the whole world was nearly not there.

It looked like an apple
or a Christmas orange:
I wanted to eat it.
I thought, It is pleasant to the eyes,
good for food,
and eating it would make men and women wise.

I could taste the juice
trickling down my throat,
my tongue smarted,
my teeth were chilled.
How sweet those mountains seemed,
how cool and tangy, the Daugava!

The Scottish poet Hugh MacDiarmid, in his essay "Poetry and Science," his own response to C. P. Snow's call for communication between scientists and artists, nicely quoted Chekhov, pledging allegiance to Chekhov's stated goal: "Familiarity with the natural sciences and with scientific methods has always kept me on my guard, and I have always tried, where it was possible, to be consistent with the facts of science." We do not want to fail to speak, or hear, any of those voices crying "I am" in the wilderness of our existence.

Many years have passed since C. P. Snow made his plea for communication between scientists and nonscientists. There are some things time has shown he was wrong about. He did not foresee the ways in which the literary canon would be stretched or revised. He did not foresee that the Soviet Union could ever be faced with economic calamity, with the result that what was left of it would wind up putting its space program up for sale to any and all buyers. He did not foresee that the "scientific revolution," which he said had followed on the industrial revolution, would be succeeded by what people are calling the "information revolution." I am sure he did not foresee that I would write this essay on a computer.

He did not foresee poets like Robert Watson and Al Zolynas, or many others, or numerous writers who would pursue an understanding of the scientific world in creative prose.

But his thesis, that scientists and nonscientists need to try to understand each other's language, is as generally valid as ever. When cultures meet, the first order of business is translation. This is as true for cultures of knowledge as for cultures of race or gender or nationality. *If we cannot even speak to one another, what good does it do us to have something to say?*

And if we speak only to ourselves, how long will we have anything new to say? We must listen to one another, if we are not to grow old telling the same anecdotes over and over, mumbling our way into graves of habit.

It is rather like two cultures meeting, then, this interchange between scientist and poet. It is rather like conversation and friendship. It is rather like strolling hand-in-hand across a shining suspension bridge flung over the endless drop into our own unknowing. Finally, here at the end of the twentieth century, it must be, for all our sakes, rather like scientist and poet accompanying each other into the twenty-first.

The Nymph Stick Insect

Observations on Poetry, Science, and Creation

With C. D. Wright, I co-edit a literary book press, Lost Roads Publishers. Lost Roads, because the map, as Jack Spicer reminds us, is not the territory. Like an anthropologist, an editor might look for the missing link, the lost species, to understand the picture, which is a picture in time. I am interested in evolution and in the proliferation of poetries. I know that only the collective assemblage of fossils, of enunciations, can establish the character of a system or an activity. We readily find Derek Walcott's poetry, but when we discover the apposing poetics of fellow islanders Kamau Brathwaite and Shake Keane, our scope widens and the meanings of Walcott's work change too. Poetry doesn't compete, Louis Zukofsky asserted; it is added to like science.

Like species, poems are not invented, but develop out of a kind of discourse, each poet tensed against another's poetics, in conversation, like casts of wormtrails in a sandstone. Our mineral attention can fill in the imprint, memorializing it. But each discovery we make only alludes to the stunning diversity, the breadth of the unrecorded, the unchampioned. When are your poetics, your politics, not implicated in another's?

History reminds us that any scientific truth is a construct and a contract with its time.

At the time when Aristotle and Theophrastus were starting a university in Greece, it was commonly assumed that stones like limonite nodules—which often had detached cores rattling around inside them—were pregnant. In one of the first treatises on the science of geology, Theophrastus claimed that lyngurium, what we now call tourmaline, a gem carved by ancient Greek jewelers into signets, is a precipitate from lynx urine. A wild lynx, in fact, produced better stones than a tame one, he had heard. Nevertheless, Theophrastus commented, only experienced searchers seemed to find lyngurium. Why? Because after a lynx passes its urine it conceals it, scraping dirt over the liquid that begins to harden, buried now, into stone.

But Theophrastus's conjecture—that animals might generate or harbor stones—is not so farfetched. Contemporary scientists tell us that lodged within the bodies of various organisms, from homing pigeons to whales, a mineral of iron and oxygen, magnetite, serves as a kind of internal compass, helping them to sense the magnetic field of the earth and so to navigate. It is said that a crayfish requires a grain of sand lodged in its "ear" before it can balance underwater. Chickens, of course, swallow pebbles for digestion. And mammals disgorge hairballs which can be mineral-hard. In fact, one impressive bezoar-stone, a fist-sized fossil hairball, dominates the living-room table of poet Clayton Eshelman.

In the thirteenth century, Albertus Magnus detailed the methods for softening gems with goat's blood, urine, and milk. To temper steel, he recommended that the metal be heated white hot and plunged repeatedly into a liquid rendered from radish juice and fluid from crushed earthworms.

With Socrates' assurance guiding his sight, Da Vinci put aside his dissecting knife and noted, wrongly, that a man's liver has five lobes.

What Theophrastus, Albertus Magnus, and Da Vinci saw corroborated *what they thought they would see* according to the prevalent assumptions of their times.

Neither good poems nor good science simply corroborate the assumption of presumed values.

Because habits of thought often determine presumptions, it can be worthwhile to keep a watch out every which way for the real thing. Hypertextual poems, poetry slams, computer-generated poems, translations: energy constantly flows into new forms.

If you want to find the second hottest body in the solar system, don't assume it will be found next to the hottest, the sun. Io, one of Jupiter's moons, kneaded between the gravitational forces of Jupiter and Europa into an ultramafic magma the consistency of olive oil, spews a lava as hot as 3,100 degrees.

How readily reality adapts to the imagination! Physicist Richard Feynman, known especially for his work with uncertainty, suggested that antiparticles might be ordinary particles traveling backward in time. His insight was elicited not by daunting mathematics but by his curiously simple-looking arrow diagrams, which suddenly made the idea seem plausible.

The diagrams themselves conceived an intuition; the scribble suggests a word. Sometimes an organ precedes its function. A structure arises, but becomes useful only after its development. Evolutionary theorists call this *exaptation*. Our brains may have developed this way. The human is the animal who lays in meaning. The poem is a structure in which meanings resonate.

There is another world, the poet Paul Éluard famously wrote, *but it is inside this one.* Quite literally. Certain bacteria live hundreds of meters within the earth's crust, taking nourishment from dissolved gases and minerals that form through the reaction of groundwater and rock. These bacteria, chemolithotrophs, have no need for solar energy. Some scientists estimate that the world inside this one, the underground biomass, might be more than double the living mass at the surface of our planet.

Perhaps we can understand now what the nineteenth-century German naturalist Alexander von Humboldt meant when he spoke of "the all-animatedness of the earth."

In his own time, Giovanni Battista Vico argued against clear, distinct, Cartesian ideas, emphasizing instead practical wisdom and *ingenium,* the power of connecting separate and diverse elements. It is his path that interests me.

Exhausted after searching for traces of hominids in northern Tanzania, Leakey's crew began clowning around, throwing elephant dung at each other. Ducking, one young man's face brushed ground that had been covered—three and a half million years ago—with a carbonite-rich volcanic ash. Rains had turned the ash into cement. There, just under his nose, he discovered the most significant Paleolithic path, the Laetoli footprints that show early hominids were fully bipedal long before they developed tool-making capabilities or an expanded brain. Twenty-seven meters of tracks left by two males, a female, and a hipparion. Poet Gary Snyder urges us to find our own way, *off the road, on the path.*

Wrote Wittgenstein, "We feel that even if all possible scientific questions be answered, the problems of life have not been touched at all."

At one time, scientific method meant that we chopped something apart and put it back together; we made a machine. That still is one scientific model, and a very successful one, for it predicts that when we do something, we will obtain certain results. But such methodology is not a universal, embracing all human experience. If we approach with a different model, we will ask different questions.

Is it Whitman who tells us that in the beauty of poems we will find "the tuft and final applause of science"? Metaphor argues against logic.

The forest, say the Pygmies, *gives us everything we need—food, clothing, shelter, warmth . . . and affection.*

In order to more fully understand death, Dr. Cabinas applied himself scientifically. Over several years, he recorded his detailed studies of the movements of decapitated bodies just after execution. What was it that he learned?

Until three hundred million years ago, fish were strictly bottom feeders within the water column. Insect wings, like those of the green nymph stick insect pinned to the wall above my desk, evolved from the moveable, articulated gill plates of ancient, aquatic insects escaping those fish. Writing is like evolution in that poems are not invented so much as they develop in the act of writing. Robert Creeley: *I see* as *I write*.

And evolution is contingent in nature. We are here by chance. John Ashbery: *It could always have been written differently.* Or, as the poet Basil Bunting put it succinctly: *Man is not end product, maggot asserts.*

We must force ourselves open to discoveries across the grain, contrary to what we "know."

In this, we may be led best by silence, an almost religious gesture of openness.

It is said that the powers of a Noh actor can be assessed simply on the basis of his *kamae*, an immobile position giving the impression of unshakeable balance and intense presence. His muscles are not tight, but neither are they relaxed. Consciousness is focused on all parts of the body simultaneously. *Kamae* is a posture open to all eventualities, virtual movement.

In the Noh play *Sekedira Komachi*, reputed to be the most difficult of all to perform, the *shite* or main actor must sit completely motionless, masked, at the front of the stage for an hour and a half, expressing corporeal intensity by his very restraint of movement.

Art is not the waging of taste only nor the exercise of argument, but like love the experience of vision, the revelation of hiddenness.

Perhaps eros is the fundamental condition of that expansion of meaning necessary to poetry, and of cognition itself. The father of Western logic, Socrates, claimed that he had only one real talent: to recognize at once the lover and the beloved.

In those very years when Socrates was making himself the gadfly of Athens, the Maya in Central America were building an extensive civilization. According to their beliefs, the world had already ended several times. It had come to an end once by fire, once by water. The final apocalypse, the one they predicted for our time, would be brought about by . . . movement.

Maybe the so-called contemporary indifference to poetry is nothing more than dread, dread that poetry is so penetrated by silence.

Because I am not silent the poems are bad. George Oppen.

Since some genes mutate at regular rates, the average number of genetic differences between species in two orders serves as a clock, showing when these animals shared a common ancestor. The common mammalian ancestor can be dated, in this way, to one hundred million years ago. This is about twenty million years before the first appearance of mammals in the fossil record.

Lost roads underlie the known roads. Lost roads and silence.

And isn't memory itself a crumpled map of lost roads crisscrossing body and brain? We are not surprised to learn that there are several memory systems: *semantic* (a kind of long-term memory for concepts), *episodic* (long-term memory for events), *short-term*, and *implicit*, or unconscious memory. Experiences of one's past are constructed by combining bits of information from several levels of knowledge.

And we know emotional and physical states strongly influence what is remembered. And our endocrinal system is clearly involved in our thinking. Wrote poet Paul Valéry: *At the end of the mind, the body; but at the end of the body, the mind.*

Unlike lyrical language, with which we were gifted, the language of science has been agreed upon. In a poem, the terms are unique, irreplaceable; they can only be quoted. But the terms for scientific language are written across an equal sign; science is predominantly expressed as a language of equivalences, of substitutions. Poetry is perhaps the ultimate challenge to any language of substitution as well as to the newspaper's language of managed reality. For me, it is the only discourse in which energy is still possible.

Once, the language of science was thought to be characterized by precision and the absence of ambiguity. Faith in the potential of a literal language bolstered assumptions of picture theories of meaning, what Bertrand Russell and Ludwig Wittgenstein were working on together, and these theories reached their peak in the doctrine of logical positivism, the notion that reality might be described through language in a testable way.

But cognition, as the poet John Keats suggested, savoring negative capability, is only the result of mental construction. Nobel physicist Richard Feynman believed in the primacy of doubt as the essence of knowing.

The objective world is not directly accessible but is constructed on the basis of constraints on our perception and on our language. Language, perception, and memory are inextricably interdependent. There is no one real world toward which science proceeds by successive approximations. As the poet William Bronk wrote: *And oh, it is always a world and not the world.* There is no neutral, objective point of view.

Look where the field of Dickcissels is swirling up into a tornado of wings. Now look down—

and you might see the swirl of mud created on the bottom of a pond by the withdrawal of an alligator snapping turtle's head. A species traceable to the early Miocene, the alligator snapper is the largest freshwater turtle. In 1937, Hall and Smith cited a specimen weighing 403 pounds caught in the Neosho River in Cherokee City, Kansas. When it would strike, its entire upper body lifted off the ground as it lunged forward like a Volkswagen.

Human muscle is packed with strands called mitochondria, which create heat in all warm-blooded animals. But mitochondria cannot contract. For this reason, reptiles, which are cold-blooded, have muscles ten times stronger than mammals.

As people who have visited me in the last two years know, I have raised from a hatchling a baby alligator snapper. But for the egg tooth and its small size, the young turtle resembles perfectly the adult. It has a reduced shell with a very small, cross-shaped plastron that exposes its underparts. Its head is large, the jaws extremely strong, and the upper beak is hooked. There are paired barbels on the chin and several irregularly shaped laminae at the under edges of the shell. The tail is long, armed above with erect bony scales. Snapping turtles have been known to bite the snouts of horses as they attempted to drink. They are the only animals ever observed to share holes, unmolested, with a bull alligator.

The primitive alligator snapping turtle, little removed from the lost road of the dinosaurs, represents a transitional group in vertebrate evolution, between aquatic fishes and terrestrial birds and mammals. As it lies underwater, it slowly opens and closes its mouth while pulsating its throat. If we added dye to the water in the tank, it would confirm the swirling currents near its mouth. The throat-pulsing increases with the length of the turtle's submersion, until the animal begins gulping water. There has been some speculation that the alligator snapping turtle, *Macroclemys temmincki*, is capable of pharyngeal respiration. Most of the time, it lies silently below the surface of the water like a cloistered monk, looking up. Because it is omnivorous, because it is open to anything and everything, all roads lead to its mouth. It waits, listening, in silence. Perhaps this is the most basic gesture of the poet.

An epigraph from D. H. Lawrence:

> The mystery of creation is the divine urge of creation.
> But it is a strange urge. It is not a mind.
> Even an artist knows that his work was never in his mind.
> He could never have thought it before it happened.
> A strange ache possessed him and he entered the struggle,
> And in the struggle with his material, in the spell of the urge,
> His work took place, it came to pass, it stood up and saluted his mind.

Poetry and Science

The Science of Poetry / The Poetry of Science

The Greek poet Constantine Cavafy is best known for his poem "Waiting for the Barbarians." The poem in Queen's English goes like this:

What are we waiting for, gathered in the market-place?

> The barbarians are to arrive today.

Why so little activity in the Senate?
Why do the senators sit without legislating?

> Because the barbarians will arrive today.
> Why should the senators bother with laws now?
> The barbarians, when they come, will do the law-making.

Why has our emperor risen so early,
and why does he sit at the largest gate of the city
on the throne, in state, wearing the crown?

> Because the barbarians will arrive today . . .

And so on. The consul and the praetors walk out in their scarlet, embroidered togas, wearing bracelets with sparkling emeralds and precious staves inlaid with silver and gold . . . because the barbarians will arrive today—and such things dazzle barbarians. Orators don't give speeches . . . because barbarians are bored by eloquence. . . . The poem concludes:

> What does this sudden uneasiness mean,
> and this confusion? (How grave the faces have become!)
> Why are the streets and squares rapidly emptying,
> and why is everyone going back home so lost in thought?
>
>> Because it is night and the barbarians have not come.
>> And some men have arrived from the frontiers
>> and they say that there are no barbarians any longer.
>
> And now, what will become of us without barbarians?
> These people were a kind of solution.[1]

Listening to so many literary orators, senators, and praetors, I have the recurring feeling that they really do believe in barbarians, in law-making barbarians, in barbarians bored by eloquence, even in barbarians threatening the sublime cultural edifices; barbarians who would be wholehearted opponents of the artist's creative complex, of the preservation of the only and truly human nature protected by the arts and humanities; barbarians who would be at the same time a kind of solution to the inborn problems of aging societies and cultures; who would at least provide an easy, silent target for traditional humanitarian emotions, passions, and conservational tendencies.

The barbarians are of course the scientists.

The romantic disjunction of head and heart is, after two hundred years, still not cured in an individual artist's mentality. The artist's primal and direct communication with the nature of man and things is still seen as an alternative and more genuine path of human creativity, opposing the analytical, cold, and cynical scientific approach.

Science is spectrum analysis: art is photosynthesis, as Karl Kraus has put it. Or, according to the Polish satirist Stanislaw Jerzy Lec, the hay smells different to the lovers than to the horses.

Let's take a look at the realm of the horses. Has it still the same constitution and structure it had during the Enlightenment and the Romantic reaction to Enlightenment? Is the scientific paradigm, that is, the apparatus of perception and the framework into which all observations are fitted,[2] unchanged throughout the last couple of centuries? Or are we confronted with a different paradigm from that which confronted the Encyclopaedists, the Rousseauians, and the Herderians?

If there is something like a "Science," that is a complex of activities creating methods for acquiring applicable information on the world, then it is not a perennial coral reef increasing by simple accretion, but a slow, frequently unnoticed transition from the First to the Second and Third Science.[3,4]

In the First Science, introduced by the ancient Greeks, the method consisted of forming axioms from which certain theorems could be deduced by the application of logical systems that would today be regarded as "philosophical" rather than "scientific." In the Renaissance, the First Science was gradually replaced by the Second. This was based on systematized observation with the naked eye or with tools developed at that time. It invented the interrogation of nature through experiments, which in turn were based on assumptions derived from direct observations, on entities conveyed by observation, on entities very similar or identical to the data of everyday sensual experience. The paradigm of the Second Science resulted in an enormous wealth of classifications, descriptions, and notions of objects and elementary forces. The Second Science is metaphorically represented by the reality of scientific libraries bulging with wisdom, aspiring to contain the world per se and the world for man, by the tons of *Handbücher* and *systemata naturae*, and by the reality of scientific laboratories where uninvolved observers ask their questions and manipulate disparate objects, dissect them and rearrange them in chains of facts and abstractions.

In the extensive mechanism of the Second Science even intensive personalities like Kelvin or Darwin bore the signs of closeness and finiteness of their fields, which resembled rather an official agenda than an abyss.

The Second Science has enriched the vocabulary by an enormous wealth of terms and denotations attributed to natural objects and technological processes. At least in this respect it had a marked positive effect on the literary mind, which followed the Second Science in the demythicization-by-denomination process, abandoning the broad notions of just trees, just flowers, or just crafts and going for concrete, specific terms. At least in the descriptive approach to objects and forces the literary mind (and culture in general) made use of the Second Science paradigm.

Nevertheless, the devitalized library and the cool, white, unimaginative laboratory—the supposed idea of the Second Science—still represent a counterpoint to what we think of as the individual Artistic Mind, deep, warm, and increasingly sophisticated in its introspection.

Frequently we find that artists believe, at least in private, that they are fundamentally opposed to this science, to inimical science that is designed to endanger their minds, their aims, and their ways of life, as well as the homeostasis of the planet. They still believe in "the Vulture whose wings are dull realities," as did Edgar Allan Poe in "the crude composition of my earliest boyhood" in 1829. They content themselves on the one hand with a subnormal understanding, of the present sciences in particular, and with a pretended general understanding of "Science" on the other, albeit they mix up science, technology, and the application of both—which is rather the consequence of the given social structure than the responsibility of sciences. Some like to understand what they believe in. Others like to believe in what they understand, says Lec. This private artistic attitude amounts to a total misunderstanding, to a kind of artistic dogmatism and, at the same time, to artistic messianism. In Lec's terms, "Every stink that fights the fan thinks it is Don Quixote."

"Humankind / Cannot bear very much reality," said T. S. Eliot.

It is astonishing how little change has occurred in the realm of lovers—in the mood and ideology of the traditional culture during the last eighty years. Almost the same controversy on culture, education, and science developed in 1882 between T. H. Huxley and Matthew Arnold and in 1959 between C. P. Snow and F. R. Leavis. In both cases the issue was the impact of science, technology, and industry on human life and on human values. But it was really Arnold who clearly understood what the Encyclopaedists, the French Revolution, and Hegel told the world, namely that Reason, Idea, or Creative Imagination had become decisive in human destiny.

Art was for Arnold a criticism of life, and literature, a central cultural act, was itself criticism of culture. But culture represented for Arnold "the best that has been thought and said in the world."[5] Consequently, the opposition of culture and science, in Snow's terms of traditional culture and scientific culture, appears to be an artificial one. The 1959 controversy is a confrontation not of two cultures but only of two autoreflections of the artistic and scientific establishments—of the artistic sensibility, and the paradigm and material consequences of the Second Science.

The controversy has hit a soil so fertile that Peter Medawar, after twenty years, protests that his essay "Science and Literature" could be taken as "yet another contribution to this idiotic debate."

However, we firmly believe with Susan Sontag that modern art is rather an extension of life than a method of knowledge and evaluation—and therefore subject to the same dynamic changes as technology and science. Hence there is very little left to argue about.

However, in this century, the paradigm of the Second Science has been broken up and is vanishing bit by bit, together with the psychological type of the private scientist with a mind prepared for the chance coming mostly late in the night. A new paradigm is emerging, that of Goodall's Third Science struggling with the "fluent" nature of things. The first step was the new development of physics where the material world was found to consist of entities basically different from anything we can experience by our senses. "The world of billiard-ball atoms existing at definite times in simple three-dimensional space dissolved into the esoteric notions of quantum mechanics and relativity, which to the unsophisticated seem most 'unnatural.'"[6] The world of living things, consisting so far of a hierarchical order of organisms, organs, cells, and functions, was dissolved into torrents of evolution, molecular interactions, realizations, and errors, all regulated by somewhat inhuman forces of genome and selection, proceeding not simply from the "lower" to the "higher" organization, but rather from the principle of minimal information to assure the preservation of that information to the principle of maximal conciseness of information. A rather "revolutionary idea" emerged "that chance and indeterminacy are among the fundamental characteristics of reality."[7]

Interest has moved toward the study of general properties of systems of information and organization. By this tendency science has enclosed many areas so far unexplored and so far regarded as being out of the scope of the hard-centered scientific approach. Paradoxes like Maxwell's demon and the mysterious neurophysiology of the human brain are within its reach. This approach reveals, too, that every scientific field touched by something like the Third Science is incomplete "and most of them—whatever the record of accomplishments over the past two hundred years—are still in the earliest stage of their starting point" (Lewis Thomas).

But, most important, the involvement of the observer in the observed holds true in general (although this notion is still under dispute among physicists). The famous Heisenberg sentence maintains: "Even in science the object of research is no longer nature itself, but man's investigation of nature."[8]

The root of the matter is not in the matter itself, as I put it in a poem.

The situation is beautifully defined by J. Robert Oppenheimer:

> We have a certain choice as to which traits of the atomic systems we wish to study and measure and which we let go; but we have not the option of doing them all. This situation, which we all recognize, sustained in [Niels] Bohr his long-held view of the human condition: that there are mutually exclusive ways of using our words, our minds, our souls, any of which is open to us, but which cannot be combined: ways as different, for example, as preparing to act and entering into a retrospective search for the reasons of action. This discovery has not, I think, penetrated into general cultural life. I wish it had; it is a good example of something that would be relevant, if only it could be understood.[9]

Last but not least, the present scientific paradigm and the organization of modern science provide a precise and lasting world memory and link distant causes with distant effects. They offer an operational framework of memory that was missing in the life of societies and in the culture.

No one of good will can fail to perceive current scientific events and their eminent role in our intellectual life. Science today "is the way of thinking much more than it is a body of knowledge," and "if science is a topic of general interest and concern—if both delights and social consequences are discussed regularly and competently in schools, the press, and at the dinner table—we have greatly improved our prospects for learning how the world really is and improving both it and us," says Carl Sagan with a grain of idealism.[10] And Lewis Thomas, who is definitely less exuberant, states: "We need science, more and better science, not for its technology, not for leisure, not even for health and longevity, but for the hope of wisdom which our kind of culture must acquire for its survival."[11]

In my essay "Science in the Unity of Culture," I referred to science as an ally of the intellect of the ordinary citizen; an ally helping him to make order out of disorganization, out of chaos, regardless of what forms these take. From the citizen's viewpoint, what we may loosely call the "intellectual functions" of science and art overlap to form a unity, with each conditioning and complementing the other.[12] This, of course, does not imply that the citizen lives all the time in the atmosphere of scientific and artistic tides; it implies only that they are within his reach when he has a chance to gasp the breath of culture.

In particular scientific disciplines that have sometimes very little in common, the barbarians may well have created disparate images of a colorless world, cold and mute, alien to any sensual evidence. But at the same time they have subjected mankind to the pressure or freedom of basic and definitive technological progress; they have provided the human mind not only with new and innovative ideas but also with new means of apperception, insight, and expression. They have also produced the worldwide system of communications and the worldwide feeling of human simultaneity, as well as producing isolated, particular scientific universes with little possibility of intercommunication and translation into a universal scientific language. The universal paradigms are present rather by implication than in an explicit form.

It was William Butler Yeats who observed in "The Return of Ulysses": "The more a poet rids his verses of heterogeneous knowledge and irrelevant analysis, and purifies his mind with elaborate art, the more does the little ritual of his verse resemble the great ritual of Nature, and become mysterious and inscrutable."[13]

So, it is not only in the science–art relationship that we suffer or believe we suffer from the lack of a common language. It is also in the art–common sense relationship. It is also within the arts themselves. Bronowski states that there is a general lack of a broad and general language in our culture.[14] But it may be suggested that this lack is merely accidental, momentary, and superficial. We may lack a common language and common sensibility, but we should be increasingly aware that we do share a common silence.

At first glimpse one might suspect that literature would be closer to the sciences than other art forms, because sciences also use words and depend on syntax for expressing their findings and formulating ideas. They have created specialized vocabularies of their own, mainly for purposes of higher precision and to approach the ultimate aim of highly formalized monolytic expression, if not a new syntax. Such a syntax has already been created by mathematicians and theoretical physicists. Writers use the same tools as scientists (except for mathematicians). They perform on the same stage, but move in the opposite direction. The sciences and poetry do not share words, they polarize them.

The assumption that a poet using scientific words, scientific vocabulary, could produce writing that would be closer to science and its spirit, without being a scientist himself is—to paraphrase Waddington—like rendering Shakespeare in the language and philosophical framework of an evening newspaper. Scientists publishing verses in the back pages of their professional magazines certainly engage in funny, witty, and graceful exercises, but are as far from poetry as poet laureates making verses on the front pages of literary magazines on the perennial merits of Poetry, verses worn out for decades or centuries. Even a gifted poet and a major scientist in one person, like the Nobel laureate for chemistry in 1981, R. Hoffman, cannot render the essence of his science in poems and writes rather about circumstances. There is no common language and there is no common network of relations and references. Actually, modern painting has in some ways come closer to the new scientific notions and paradigms, precisely because a painter's vocabulary, colors, shapes, and dimensions are not congruent to the scientist's vocabulary. Their vocabularies are not mutually exclusive, but complementary.

Many present scientific disciplines are represented by their wording, or are embodied in the words, or are even seen as the thing said. Poetry is not the thing said, but a way of saying it (A. E. Housman).

For the sciences, words are an auxiliary tool. In the development of modern poetry words themselves turn into objects, sometimes *objets trouvés*. For William Carlos Williams, "The poem is made of things—on a field." Thus the poem dwells in a new space and a new time and is due in Williams's example to a "strange arithmetic or chemistry of art: '—to dissect away / the block and leave / a separate metal: / hydrogen / the flame, helium the / pregnant ash.'"[15] To paraphrase Heisenberg, the object of poetic research is no longer nature itself, but man's use of words. Hence poetry moves ahead, paralleling the scientific paradigm in the realm of language, into areas less comprehensible for a reader accustomed to forming coherent mental pictures from the sequence of phrases, that is to say, accustomed to the commonplace or scientific use of words.

There may be an essential trait involved: the basis of any art, at least in a modern sense, is exactly that which cannot be recorded by this art's specific means, that which surpasses them. The basis of poetry is the unpronounceable, the basis of a picture is the unpaintable, the basis of music is the unplayable, and the basis of drama is hidden beyond the action. Perhaps art is based on the immanent inadequacy of its means, while science insists on the adequacy, or at least the temporary adequacy, of its means. Art is a binding inadequacy and therefore it is close to life. Science is a binding adequacy, limited by its time and space. Science has to say everything. Art that would say everything would be its own grave, as shown by pseudo-art, which always contains instructions for the consumer and formulates the final and obligatory commonplace notions.

In the use of words, poetry is the reverse of the sciences. Sciences bar all secondary factors associated with writing or speaking; they are based on a single logical meaning of the sentence or of the word. In poetry, very definite thoughts occur, but they are not and cannot be expressed by words stripped of secondary factors (graphic, phonetic) and especially by words chosen so as to bar all possibilities except one. On the contrary, poetry tries for as many possible meanings and interactions between words and thoughts as it can. This is not only for its inner freedom, but also for the sake of communication with readers, for their own freedom. The poet uses "these words because the interests whose movement is the growth of the poem combine to bring them, just in this form, into consciousness as a means of ordering, controlling, and consolidating the uttered experience of which they are themselves a main part." The experience or, more broadly put, the tide of impulses "sweeping through the mind, is the source and the sanction of the words."[16] For the reader, the words of the poem are meant to reproduce similar, analogous, or parallel plays of feelings, thoughts, and interests, putting him for a while into a similar, analogous, or related inner situation, leading to his particular response. Why this should happen, says Richards, is the mystery of communication. Who knows how often it happens per book, per reading, or per lifetime. Definitely not as frequently as we pretend.

With the increasing sophistication and matter-of-factness of its actual and potential readership, the essential poetic communication or triggering needs fewer words and more condensation in Pound's sense (*dichten = condensare*).

One of the functions of words in a poem is to make pseudo-statements in Richards's terms. The sole function of words in the scientific paper is to make statements that are not an end in themselves, but the matter of verification for future experimentation or for a present or presented theory. The "truth" of poetic statements is acceptable or verifiable by some attitude, within the framework of the mood, style, and reference of the poem. By reference I mean the relationship to a system of routine statements, to common sense, and to the literary traditions and contexts. "The poetic approach evidently limits the framework of possible consequences into which the pseudo-statement is taken. For the scientific approach this framework is unlimited. Any and every consequence is relevant."[17]

Interestingly, at least in my mind, which may be affected by my profession, some essential scientific notions, postulates, laws, some basic stones of the scientific syntax cannot be modified, cannot be transformed into pseudo-statements even when used in a poem. The poem too has to keep some bones of the scientific skeleton of the world. The point is illustrated in my prose poem "Žito the Magician":

> To amuse His Royal Majesty he will change water into wine. Frogs into footmen. Beetles into bailiffs. And make a minister out of a rat. He bows, and daisies grow from his finger-tips. And a talking bird sits on his shoulder.
>
> There.
>
> Think up something else, demands His Royal Majesty. Think up a black star. So he thinks up a black star. Think up dry water. So he thinks up dry water. Think up a river bound with straw-bands. So he does.
>
> There.
>
> Then along comes a student and asks: Think up sine alpha greater than one.
>
> And Žito grows pale and sad: Terribly sorry. Sine is between plus one and minus one. Nothing you can do about that.
>
> And he leaves the great royal empire, quietly weaves his way through the throng of courtiers, to his home in a nutshell.[18]

So, in the use of words and statements, poetry and science move in different and almost opposite directions. But they do not aim, in my mind, for opposite ends. One of them is a humility that resists the onslaughts of powerful, prevailing imbecility, verbal or otherwise.

The aim of a scientific communication is to convey unequivocal information about one facet of a particular aspect of reality to the reader, and to the collective, anonymous thesaurus of scientific data. The aim of poetic communication is to introduce a related feeling or grasp of the one aspect of the human condition to the reader, or to the collective mind of cultural consciousness. As person-to-person messages, both kinds of communication involve a definite time of the full intellectual or intellectual-emotional presence. In addition, both are concerned with the establishment of a lasting memory, of intellectual or intellectual-emotional debris in the individual mind and in the collective mind of culture. And both the scientific and poetic communications are a function of condensation of meanings, of the net weight of meaning per word, of inner and immanent intensity. Opposed to other written communications, they are—at their best— concentrates, time-saving devices. I have been repeatedly intrigued by hearing from scientific colleagues that they do read poetry, because it is short, instantaneous, and rewarding on the spot, just as a good scientific paper should be.

And the notion of the specific high inner intensity shared by the scientific and poetic communication leads me to suggest that there is another common trait: the goal of gravitational force of sudden revelation, discovery or statement with a predictive value. Here we are actually referring more to the very scientific action than to the communication, and at the same time to the act of writing rather than to the completed poem. But we must not forget that even the present form of scientific papers is based on a proven narrative structure of introduction, technical elaboration, and almost instantaneous presentation of the findings where the graphic, numerical, or condensed textual statements sometimes attain the value of a revealing metaphor.

In some sciences, which are still fully dependent on the traditional syntax, a conscious application of some sophisticated literary forms may occasionally occur. So a form of platonic dialogue between Prof.

Soma (the name standing for the advocates of a somatic mutation theory) and Prof. Line (for germinal line theory) has been chosen by F. C. Osher and W. C. Neal for an impressive confrontation of the theories of generation of diversity (GOD) in immunological recognition. The article was published among "normal" scientific communications in *Cellular Immunology* (17:552, 1975). I'd even suggest that in these sciences the aesthetic value of the literary communication still counts, and may become a noticeable quality. George Orwell may have been right when he remarked: "Above the level of a railway guide, no book is quite free from aesthetic considerations."

Comparing good scientific stuff with boring repetitive articles about minor problems as well as comparing accomplished poems with boring non-communicative stanza after stanza, it can be stated that the common denominator of quality, of goodness, is in both cases the notion of a little discovery, a discovery that is going to stay and attract our attention also in the future, in other situations, and in different contexts. And the longing to make the little discovery and prediction is, I feel, the primary motivation of both the scientific and poetic action. William Carlos Williams: "Invent (if you can) discover or / nothing is clear—will surmount / the drumming in your head."

So too the Czech modernist poet Vítězslav Nezval: "And the aesthetic rule that once caused a radical overthrow in art may be at other times a burden for inspiration, a galley lead. Therefore the principal marker of art which provokes our interest is the novelty" (1930).

If the result is good, and this may happen at times, the great feeling is conveyed even to the reader of the scientific report. William Carlos Williams has remarked in a poem: "We / have / microscopic anatomy / of the whale. This is / reassuring." I don't think that this poem is so ironic. For Williams has written too: "So much depends / upon / a red wheel / barrow," and this is taken seriously by everybody.

Or in an example from a recent scientific event: S. T. Peale, P. M. Cassen, and R. T. Reynolds published in *Science* (2 March 1979) a paper indicating that Jupiter's gravity, tugging the near side of Jupiter's satellite Io harder than the far side, would cause the interior of Io to yield and create friction and heating, the accumulated heat being sufficient to melt the core, so that widespread volcanism can be expected. They said: "Voyager images of Io may reveal evidence for a planetary structure dramatically different from any previously observed." Three days thereafter Voyager I reached Jupiter and transmitted pictures of Io's yellow, orange, and white surface shaped by recent volcanic activity and, later, clouds rising from a giant volcano. The human satisfaction one obtains from this episode equals the satisfaction from a great poem; the poetic quality is in the elegance of the prediction and in the coincidence of timing of the publication and the Voyager I success. No poetic qualities could be found in the paper itself.

On the contrary, an idea that appears extremely attractive in its human message, in its face value, and in its wording happens to be very dangerous and misleading in the scientific context. A recent example occurs to me. Somebody investigated the reason for frequent miscarriages in an area where men used to drag heavily loaded ships by ropes. The author examined the miscarried fetuses and found that they were preponderantly of male sex, tended to turn away from the placenta, and held the umbilical cords in their hands and over their shoulder, as if they were ropes. This is definitely a very poetic idea. Confronted by the valid genetic notions on the inheritance of adaptive qualities, the idea is a disaster and the observation may be rather an example of wishful thinking and jumping to conclusions than of a scientific hard or soft fact. Human approaches do not count in science. The moral and aesthetic values emerge at the very beginning and at the very end of the scientific activity, not in its mechanism.

What, then, is the difference or the likeness of the human experience in the very act of science-making and poetry-making? Are there common roots in the so-called creative impulse, and are there common enjoyments in these two activities that we have described as basically different in the uses of words and handling of meanings?

Let us follow the single steps schematically:

1. Decision to act. In the lab, there is hardly ever the chance to start something new, to ask a purely personal, independent question. What one starts with is a heavy burden of accumulated literature that is supposed to be known. The statement of the question is determined

by the literature, by the hard facts, and by the gaps. However, the question still may be personal, since it depends also on one's own interests, instincts for what may be important, the history of the work done (the profile of the lab), and the self-evaluation (what can I do with my skills, what can I afford with the given intellectual capacities and with the given tools?). After many twists and revisions, suddenly the point appears: this hasn't been done yet, this is technically feasible, this is going to work, and this may lead to some yes or no answers. The emergence of the theme has a definite emotional quality and brings some sort of a recurrent enthusiasm, which one experiences any time one gets to the bench and to the work.

A sort of subacute or chronic inspiration, tension, hope, and fear. Like a gastric ulcer, which you don't speak about.

Now the poem: I cannot give here, of course, a generally valid psychological pattern. I have to refer to my own experience and rely on the vivisection of my own writing. The statement or, better, feeling of the theme is primarily here; the confrontation with the work done by the subject and by the others is secondary. The theme appears to me as a general metaphor, as a shift from the obvious to the parareal. Its emergence implies the instincts for self-evaluation and personal style. What is strongly felt is again that . . . yes, this is going to work, this may work, if . . . this may lead to a poem. The emergence of the theme is at times the function of a definite emotional state that appears to be both the trigger and the driving and unifying force. At any rate, the emergence of the theme is connected with the feelings of elation, pain, relief, and with the same sort of acute enthusiasm that keeps one at work, even if it is not done at once.

Something like controlled heart insufficiency, which you freely advertise.

The basic difference between the emergence of the scientific theme and the poem theme is the notion and necessity of purification, definition, and linearity in the former, and the notion of necessity of the openness, ramification-potential, and multilevel interaction in the latter. The scientific theme implies as much light as possible, the poetic one as many shadows as possible. If they are not here, they must be created, opened, found in the course of the poem. The basic likeness of both activities is the agreeable experience of the self, of the interior functioning, or even well-functioning machine. If this sounds heretical for poetry, I would refer to William Carlos Williams: The poem is a machine made of words.

The agreeable experience may be better denoted as the realization of inner freedom, of the freedom of choice, of one of the very few moments of existential freedom. I tried to define this feeling, common to the finding of the way in the lab and to the finding of the way of the poem, in my piece "On the Origin of Legal Power":

> This time,
> when houses sit on eggs
> of the little painted Easter death
> and the symphony orchestra
> is dug in behind the bushes,
>
> when bassoons and trombones
> loom up on the road,
> asking for alms bigger than
> the live weight of the body,
>
> and he, listening to
> the inner unison we used to know by heart,
> to the tempest-in-the-teapot,
> to this in-spite-of-all-of-that,
>
> does not recognize the big city
> because of the little flame,
> does realize the fatigue of the mountain mass
> face to face with a falling stone
>
> and
> at least this time
> when asked, replies,
>
> Yes, I can.
>
> And goes
> the way of the flute.

2. Doing it. In the lab, doing it is so complicated that it can be described in the simplest terms. In one of the few poems where I could really render something from the laboratory experience, I said:

> You ask the secret.
> It has just one name:
> again . . .

"Doing it," working in the lab, requires a lot of self-restraint and discipline, of mastering momentary impulses for variations and deviations of the work, of tolerance for pitfalls and uncertainties, for the provisorial and not-yet-accomplished, for boring repetitions of the same step, for a pedantic order of actions and thoughts. It is at times a lonely, stubborn, and defensive endeavor: there are always, as S. J. Lec says, some Eskimos around who would advise the inhabitants of the Congo what to do during the hot summer. To this end, let me quote my poem "The Truth":

> He left, infallible, the door itself
> was bruised as he
> hit the mark,
>
> We two sat awhile
> the figures in the protocols
> staring at us like
> green huge-headed beetles
> out of the crevices of evening.
>
> The books stretched
> their spines,
>
> the balance weighed just for the fun of it
> and the glass beads in the necklace
> of the god of sleep whispered together
> in the scales.
>
> "Have you ever been right?" one of us asked.
> "I haven't."

Then we counted on.
It was late
And outside the smoky town, frosty and purple
climbed to the stars.[19]

Now, "doing the poem" involves psychological mechanisms that I am tempted to describe in almost analogous terms. Metaphorically, I would say, it means to run the lab in the mind, with discipline, with the utmost sense of order and style, allowing for new incoming associations and notions only if they keep to the preconceived framework of possible consequences. William Carlos Williams went as far as: "This combination of order with discovery, with exploration and revelation, the vigor of sensual stimulation, is of the essence of art."[20] The whole process is happening in one spot and in one time, or at least in one unique inner atmosphere that may occur at different times. It feels rather as if "it is being done" or "it is doing it" than "I am doing it."

The pitfalls and errors in lab work can be made good and eradicated by repetitions. The pitfalls and errors in the poem lead more frequently to wreckage and abandonment. However, both activities involve the basic risk of possible definitive losing, up to the moment when one suddenly discovers that it works, in spite of all that.

3. "Finding it," the moment of success, or at least what one takes to be the proof of fulfillment, the experience of the little discovery, which is virtually identical when looking into the microscope and seeing the expected (or at times the unexpected but meaningful) and when looking at the nascent organism of the poem. The emotional, aesthetic, and existential value is the same. It is one of the few real joys in life.

A strong feeling of reality. So strong that I've never dared describe it. Maybe also because I do not have enough personal experience with this moment. Neither in the lab. Nor in poetry.

But in any case, I feel compelled by all that I know to answer the above-stated question positively. Yes, there is a common root of so-called creativity; there is the same experience of fulfillment and inner reward. Therefore I could never quite understand people asking,

How can you do both these things that are basically so different? They are technically different, technically at opposite poles of the application of language, but emanate from the same deep level of the human urge, and the application of all available forces.

So far, I've tried to describe science-making and poem-making as if one was alone with the theme, alone with the work, alone with the result. In reality, one is at almost all times deeply immersed in the collective process of life and survival, caring and worrying, winning and losing. There is no such thing as a "scientist," and there is no such thing as a "poet". One can pretend it, one may play the role, but the essence of "being it" is realized only in the rare moments described. I tried to elaborate on this in "Conversation with a Poet":

You are a poet? Yes, I am.
How do you know?
    I have written a poem.
When you wrote the poem, it meant you were a poet. But now?
    I shall write another poem some day.
Then you may again be a poet. But how will you know that it really is a poem?
    It will be just like the last one.

In that case it will certainly not be a poem. A poem exists only once— it cannot be the same again.
    I mean it will be just as good.

But you cannot mean that. The goodness of a poem exists only once and does not depend on you but on circumstances.
    I imagine the circumstances will be the same.

If that is your opinion, you never were a poet and never will be. Why, then, do you think you are a poet?
    Well, I really don't know . . .
    But who are you?

I can't be in other people's skin and I can't judge; but for myself, I would say that I have spent 95 percent of my time and energy in fighting my way through the wild vegetation of circumstances, looking for the tiny spots, for the little clearing where I eventually could really work, write, or do research, albeit the second happens to be my profession.

Why, then, should it make so much difference, being the poet and being the scientist, when 95 percent of our time we are really secretaries, telephonists, passers-by, carpenters, plumbers, privileged and underprivileged citizens, waiting patrons, applicants, household maids, clerks, commuters, offenders, listeners, drivers, runners, patients, losers, subjects, and shadows?

There is a tremendous amount of amateurism in everyday life and in professional life. The tension between the husks of unprofessional tasks and burdens and the kernels of professionalism is the most frequent tension in our experience. Our hard-centered scientific approach, as well as our soft-centered artistic approach, appears to be of little use in solving both the profane and the deepest troubles of our lives in moments of urgent need, alarm, crisis, and desolation.

We pretend to live inside a world-fruit of our creativity and culture. But in fact our work happens to be a tiny, subtle, at times permeating, but most of the time confined domain in a world and in an age dominated by the giants of management and manipulation, by untamed autonomous superstructures that look down at us as if at an easily manageable microbial culture.

And this is the last aspect of reality where there is a total amalgamation of science and poetry: some sort of actual or potential hope in the world of autarchic actions. And this is exactly what we quoted from Oppenheimer: "mutually exclusive ways of using our words ... minds ... souls ... ways as different ... as preparing to act and entering into retrospective search for the reasons for action."

Let me conclude, therefore, with my "Brief Reflection on the Test Tube":

> You take
>> a bit of fire, a bit of water,
>> a bit of rabbit or tree,
>> or any little piece of man,
>> you mix it, shake well, cork it up,
>> put it in a warm place, in darkness, in light, in frost,

leave it alone for awhile—
though things don't leave you alone—
and that's the whole point.

And then
you have a look—and it grows,
a little sea, a little volcano,
a little tree, a little heart, a little brain,
so small you don't hear it pleads
to be let out,
and that's the whole point, not to hear.

Then you go
and record it, all the minuses or
all the pluses, some with an exclamation-mark,
all the zeros, or all the numbers, some with an exclamation-mark,
and the point is that the test tube
is an instrument for changing question- into exclamation-marks,

And the point is
that for the moment you forget
you yourselves are

In the test tube.

NOTES

1. E. Keeley, P. Sherrard, *Six Poets of Modern Greece* (London, 1960).

2. T. C. Kuhn, *The Structure of Scientific Revolutions* (Chicago, 1962).

3. M. C. Goodall, *Science and the Politician* (Cambridge, Mass., 1965).

4. C. H. Waddington, *Behind Appearance* (Cambridge, Mass., 1970).

5. L. Trilling, *Beyond Culture: Essays on Literature and Learning* (London, 1958).

6. Waddington, *Behind Appearance*.

7. Trilling, *Beyond Culture*.

8. W. Heisenberg, *The Physicist's Conception of Nature* (London, 1958).

9. J. Robert Oppenheimer, *Some Reflections on the Romance of Science and Culture* (Chapel Hill, 1960).

10. Carl Sagan, *Broca's Brain: Reflections on the Romance of Science* (New York, 1979).

11. Lewis Thomas, *The Medusa and the Snail: More Notes of a Biology Watcher* (New York, 1979).

12. M. Holub, "Science in the Unity of Culture," *Impact of Science on Society* 20.151 (1970).

13. W. B. Yeats, *Ideas of Good and Evil* (London, 1903).

14. J. Bronowski, *The Common Sense of Science* (Melbourne, 1951).

15. J. Hillis Miller, *Poets of Reality: Six Twentieth-Century Poets* (Cambridge, Mass., 1965).

16. I. A. Richards, *Poetries and Sciences* (New York, 1970).

17. Ibid.

18. M. Holub, *Selected Poems,* trans. I. Milner & G. Theiner (Harmondsworth, 1967).

19. Ibid.

20. Ibid.

EMILY GROSHOLZ

Poetry and Science in America

Poetry and science are opposed, even hostile, enterprises. The regulative ideals of science demand a perspective on reality that abstracts from the accidents of human perception and perhaps (if it's possible) cognition. And they demand language whose descriptions are precise and unambiguous. Poetry, by contrast, describes human actions that inspire pity, fear, and laughter, in ambiguous, image-laden, and figurative language. Their conflicting claims on truth are sometimes negotiated by granting inhuman nature to science, and moral and historical human culture to poetry. Yet poetry often wishes to speak authoritatively about nature; and science tries to annex human behavior and social institutions as domains of study. On these disputed topics, science accuses poetry of saying nothing determinate and useful, and poetry accuses science of covering over its own human attachments and need for conceptual figures.

This conflict is not a misunderstanding; it expresses a real bifurcation in human knowledge and, if one may say so, reality, which can never be overcome. And that inevitable fault in things renders attempts by either poetry or science to master the other pointless, and also gives poetry an advantage. For the fault in things makes the world a highly ambiguous place, and poetry is at home with ambiguity.

So reality (and the language and knowledge that accord with it) is at once scientific and poetic, without hope of reconciliation. But that doesn't mean that poetry should steer clear of science. On the contrary: poetry's interest in, indebtedness to, and hostility toward science are rich sources of poetic invention, as the record of twentieth-century poetry testifies.

Nature and culture are opposed terms. Yet, in a secondary sense, culture (whatever else it is) is an aspect of nature, arising out of and existing within it. Thus poets cannot simply restrict themselves to human action; they must pronounce upon the wider sphere of nature in which human action is implicated. An American poet writing at the turn of the millennium cannot escape some kind of confrontation with science and its vision of the natural order.

Moreover, science can be taken up with oblique and cheerful naiveté by the poet, and raided as one more repository of interesting cultural artifacts. Despite, and sometimes because of, its own regulative ideals, science generates striking images and metaphors, rich and novel language, acts of heroism and evil, and strangely suggestive concepts; and it has opened up new cosmologies and cosmogonies that poets can hardly ignore. In this respect, it would be better for poetry as a whole if poets had stronger scientific educations, so that they could more often profit from these wonderful resources.

Finally, as part of its moral responsibility in the modern world, poetry has to criticize science and reassert (in poetry that is beautiful and wise) the primacy of its own claim to certain domains along reality's great fault. One strategy of American poets has been to hand the discursive, systematic, and objective over to science, and to retreat into poetry that is relentlessly subjective, hermetic, and fragmentary. In my opinion, this is as much an abdication of the rights and duties of poetry as refusing to criticize science for its inherent risks that threaten both nature and culture. This strategy also keeps poets from appreciating the moral virtues that scientific objectivity and systematicity help to foster, as well as the important practical role of the discursive. And it disables poets' ability to find readers and extend their art.

Of course, one might be a bit more playful and less severe and tolerate hyper-subjectivity as a poetic mode, which the opposition between poetry and science always leaves open as a possibility. Its inverse, fed by a similar desire to realize a rhetorical (and metaphysical) possibility, is hyper-objectivity, poetry that aims for the inhuman detachment of science. Lucretius is the wellspring of that mode, and its twentieth-century exponents were Robinson Jeffers, Robert Frost, and (a scholar of both Jeffers and Frost) Radcliffe Squires.

Despite their inevitable conflict, poetry and science have one important thing in common: they are both representations. Their practitioners are extremely self-conscious of their role as representers, for the fact of representation is essential to their pursuit of truth, bifurcated as it is. The scientist puts forward conceptual models and experiments; the dramatic poet mounts a play in a theater. Because poets present not reality but a representation, they achieve universality and catharsis, the purification of experience; because scientists present not reality but a representation, they achieve universality and explanation, the rationalization of experience. Strangely enough, it is our ability to stand at one remove from experience that lets us understand experience. Because we can interrupt, negate, recast, falsify, and even betray reality, reality is ours. Once again, here poetry seems to have an edge on science, for poetry is at home with original sin and redemption, the problem of evil and the conundrum of hope.

The language of science is mathematics, and mathematics is an instrument of ontological neutralization: it treats different kinds of things as if they were just the same, in virtue of shared mathematical structure. This apparent indifference to kinds goes along with an indifference to individuals, or rather an incapacity to refer to individuals: mathematics never comes down to their level, but only, if anywhere, to equivalence classes. Poets, who are attached in an ambiguous way to concrete particulars, find the mathematization of reality unsettling, fascinating, open to criticism, and at the very least worthy of comment.

In Howard Nemerov's "Seeing Things," the title itself suggests the poet's mixed feelings: does science allow us to see things, things as they really are, or to "see things" in the sense intended when, confronted by a mirage or ghost, someone says, "I must be seeing things"?

Close as I ever came to seeing things
The way the physicists say things really are
Was out on Sudbury Marsh one summer eve
When a silhouetted tree against the sun
Seemed at my sudden glance to be afire:
A black and boiling smoke made all its shape.

Binoculars resolved the enciphered sight
To make it clear the smoke was a cloud of gnats,
Their millions doing such a steady dance
As by the motion of the many made the one
Shape constant and kept it so in both the forms
I'd thought to see, the fire and the tree.

Strike through the mask? you find another mask,
Mirroring mirrors by analogy
Make visible. I watched till the greater smoke
Of night engulfed the other, standing out
On the marsh amid a hundred hidden streams
Meandering down from Concord to the sea.[1]

Versifying the thought of his Greek predecessors Democritus and Epicurus, the Latin poet Lucretius in the first century B.C. declared that the way things really are, if we could but strike through the mask of phenomena, is a rain of atoms in the void. During the seventeenth century, almost all the great natural philosophers (Galileo, Descartes, Locke) agreed that the true qualities of things were primary qualities, those that could be quantified, and not secondary qualities, those the senses suggest things have. The seventeenth-century thinkers played metaphysically with some version of atomism, revived and recast by classicizing Renaissance scholars. In the twentieth century, the physicist Sir Arthur Stanley Eddington suggested that we should accustom ourselves to the thought that what the senses tell us is a solid table is really a volume of empty space with invisible particles whizzing through it.

Nemerov embodies these abstract considerations at the same time that he acknowledges their abstraction, and the abstractness of his own response to them. Nemerov, the supreme ironist, reverses and reverses his perceptions in the light of science until finally, and as if inevitably, ironic skepticism in the service of embodiment and particularity wins out over scientific dictum.

Science says the senses deceive us; Nemerov, the beholder in the poem, starts out by stating that he was deceived by his senses. Unable to resolve so much detail at a distance, he mistook a "cloud" of gnats for a burning tree (a macroscopic natural object, and a biblical emblem as well): "a black and boiling smoke made all its shape." But he corrects his error with binoculars (offspring of Galileo's telescope, key to so many locked-up truths in the seventeenth century), and discovers what is really there: a "cloud" of gnats masquerading as a fiery tree or the divine numen, a many that seems to be one only in virtue of a furious, ceaseless motion that expresses its manyness: "a steady dance." Just so the scientist discovers that macroscopic objects are really only a steady dance of the many, atomic and sub-atomic particles (or fields, or folds in space), where the one has been reduced to the mere steadiness of the dance: a function, a pattern, a regularity. Things fall apart.

The last stanza, however, works ironically against the drift of the first two. Gnats, after all, are insects, macroscopic organisms that science in its present reductive trend from zoology and botany to biochemistry can only wish to analyze further, to decompose into another "cloud" of elaborate carbon-based molecules, which themselves will then demand analysis. Science has opened the floodgates of the many; its frail unities, mere mathematical forms and formulae, continually dissolve to multiplicity. Whatever science arrives at, whenever science claims to show the way things really are, its idiom and its method betray its claim to closure: for its things, its unities, always dissolve.

"Strike through the mask? you find another mask / [that] mirroring mirrors by analogy / make visible." Nemerov has chosen his analogies very carefully so that they will be sure to exhibit the mask behind the mask behind the mask, the hall of mirrors, the groundlessness of science's enterprise. The smoke of gnats, mimicking the smoke of fire, recalling the smoke of Moses' burning bush, dancing like the smoke of molecules, is engulfed by "the greater smoke of night." Certainly, for Nemerov the ironist, the sensory, analogical demonstration of groundlessness does not discredit science. But it prevents science from laying claim to ultimate description. Nemerov knows perfectly well where he is: not in the midst of some vortex in the void, but on Sudbury Marsh, "amid a hundred hidden streams / Meandering down from Concord to the sea." And he knows what he has seen: night engulfing all visible things, which nonetheless abide, hidden, meandering.

Mathematics, however, has a perennial attraction for the poet, for mathematics is a treasury of beautiful forms that are ideal, and so transcendent and regulative. Regarded that way, the fragile unities it imposes can stand for more robust, though less perfect kinds of unity, like the unit that love bestows on and duty requires of the meandering of everyday life. This insight governs the "Double Sonnet for Minimalists," which Mona Van Duyn has subjected to the severe constraints of dimeter and close rhyme.

The severity of the form should remind us that mathematics bears on poetry not only by analogy, but directly through metrics. Metrics is the science of poetry, and it would be healthy for poetry if that science were more widely and astutely studied. Some rules we follow freely to organize and enrich our lives, or our poems.

> The spiral shell
> apes creamhorns of smog,
> Dalmation, quenelle
> or frosted hedgehog,
> yet is obsessed
> by a single thought
> that its inner guest
> is strictly taught.

When the self that grew
to follow its rule
is gone, and it's through,
vacant, fanciful,

its thought will find
Fibonacci's mind.[2]

The two sonnets together celebrate the two-component sea snail, through each of its parts sequentially, and through the life and death of each part. The first sonnet considers the shell. Its spiral form aligns it in the poet's imagination, accidentally and essentially, with other creatures and phenomena, whirlwinds and small mammals. But its inherent purpose and living concern is to protect, and by that very function to shape, its gastropod inhabitant, and that "obsession" makes it particular.

Then the death of the shell's fleshly counterpart in effect liberates it into the empty, universal, imaginative realm of mathematics, the domain discovered by Greek geometers and the early number theorist Leonardo Fibonacci. The greatest result in his *Liber abaci* is an infinite sequence of numbers where each term after the first two is the sum of the two terms immediately preceding it; it has many beautiful applications, including organic growth like that of snail shells. In the heaven of mathematics, the shell is in a sense reunited with the other creatures with which the poet had at first associated it, in a zoo or garden of spiral-bearers, for the poet has as much right to beautiful form as the mathematician. The sacrifice is individuality; the gain is deathlessness and a certain community.

Of course, an abandoned shell, like a bone, is a concrete particular, doomed to dissolution and self-enclosure. The transformation it undergoes in the first sonnet is the poet's magic, as she thinks it and accords it thought: "its thought will find / Fibonacci's mind." The poet makes it stand for one of the intuitively beautiful universals of mathematics, as the latter are so often made to stand for divinity, whatever it is that transcends our reality not just abstractly, but concretely. And after all, a spiral shell, like a cubical crystal or a hexagonal honeycomb cell, wears the mathematical form it instantiates on its face, and so serves the poet's purposes especially well.

What about the inhabitant, the snail at the heart of the shell, who is the shell's heart and purpose?

> That fragile slug,
> bloodless, unborn,
> till it knows the hug
> of love's tutoring form,
> whose life, upstart
> in deep, is to learn
> to follow the art
> of turn and return,
> when dead, for the dense
> casts up no clue
> to the infinite sequence
> it submitted to.
>
> May its bright ghost reach
> the right heart's beach.[3]

As Mona Van Duyn remarks in a footnote, a slug without a shell is never spiral; it only gets that shape in virtue of its shell. Once again, the poet makes the shell a rule of order, but in this sonnet the rule is not mere mathematics, but the rule of love. The shift makes poetic sense because what is formed by the shell is a sentient, growing organism; love constrains, but its constraint is also an embrace that we feel and grow into. And love holds the past, present, and future together in a peculiarly forceful and well-formed fashion: the temporal trajectory of love is spiral. Lovers learn "to follow the art / of turn and return."

Finally, according to Van Duyn, death allows the little ghost of the snail to run free of its slug-body that in itself never knew, but only submitted to, a spiral form. Then the transmuted snail and its elevated shell may come together again, in the mind of Fibonacci, perhaps, or the poet's heart, two shores of the same dividing sea.

Still, this reunion seems far from the hug, the turn and return of human love. The transcendence and redemption offered by mathematical science may leave a reader exalted but somehow unconsoled, indeed, disconsolate. Robert Morgan, in his poem "Radiation Pressure," writes of light using scientific vocabulary and concepts, and thereby achieves a gentle, almost romantic irony that utterly inverts the old metaphors of light in love poetry. He represents light as an inhuman force that sweeps all things before it. For science tells us light is a stream of photons that, while they may not have mass, yet have momentum, and so exert force on what they encounter.

> Though in our slow world of friction
> and gravity we hardly feel it,
> light presses on the things it hits,
> pouring on a stream of photons
> against each surface, raining down
> forever on each face and facet,
> propelling bodies in deep space,
> beyond significant gravity,
> away from the white source. They flee
> the emanation, as radiance
> pushes down and washes all matter
> in its way, sweeping dust and crystal,
> even little moons and planets,
> toward darkness, clearing way for
> solar wind to thrill without
> obstruction. Though here where sunlight
> touches a hand or lip we feel
> only slightest pressure, a kiss,
> a breath come across the mighty
> distances to urge away, while
> we're stayed by our very sadness.[4]

When we experience light as a kiss or a breath, as like the slight pressure one lover exerts on the hand or lip of another, we could not be more deeply mistaken. For light, correctly understood, that is, as understood by science, is the agent of darkness and estrangement, pushing everything "away from the white source." Little by little, light triumphs over matter, but science makes it plain that this triumph is perdition, an emptiness where solar wind can "thrill without obstruction." Science unmasks our perception and our common metaphors.

And yet, our experience stubbornly resists not science so much as the force science warns us about, the huge wind of light that threatens to carry us away. "We're stayed by our very sadness." We stand fast because we are slow, tractional, heavy, and sad. We are attached to our world, our memories, each other, our regret for what might have been but never will be, our puzzling hope, our bodies; and so we will not be urged away from life. Science may demonstrate to us that we are governed by necessity, that our perceptions and metaphors of freedom are illusory; but we are not moved. Sunlight still kisses our lips, even those of the scientist and the educated amateur who are quite convinced that a photon has momentum.

Science, like any rationalist system, threatens us with necessity. And, like any materialist system, it threatens us with ghostliness. Its matter is mathematical, impalpable, invisible, and so stands in problematic relation to the world and body that is ours. In the poem "Inertia," Morgan once again uses the language of science to articulate our stubborn resistance to the entailments of science.

> There is such a languor to matter,
> every mass asserting presence
> while soaring in its stasis.
> Electrons spin and molecules
> twitch, yet the material resists
> all change of direction, defends
> its momentum and moment, in
> the reverie of substance, the
> immobility and dream of
> the body's authority of weight,
> remaining undisturbed, by poise
> of precedence, occupation,
> reluctant as a bear to wake
> from the immanence and ponder,
> the gravity of mere artlessness.[5]

"The reverie of substance" has for two thousand years been the philosophers' way of acknowledging and pondering the unity of things, of thought, and of individuals. Aristotle used it against the congeries of Democritus, and Kant used it against the corrosive skepticism of Hume. The presence of other creatures that inspires in us such respect, fear, and love, is due *inter alia* to body's authority, its poise, stasis, moment, occupation. Indeed, the seventeenth-century scientists expressed their respect for the bear of the body in its cave of immanence, by the words they chose to name the fundamental concepts of mechanics.

The necessitarian and ghostly-materialist metaphysics that tends so persistently to accompany science wakens great anxiety in many poets. But not in a few, it calls up an emotion more like anger. The poet Eleanor Wilner has questioned and refashioned many of the myths that organize our culture, its metaphysics, and the practical consequences that flow therefrom, half-accidentally, half-essentially. In her poem "The Literal = The Abstract: A Demonstration," she contests the ghostliness of science, and finds its necessities truly fatal.

> After all those swerving arcs in air,
> the dance of shadows like an answer
> from the ground, and all the dear
> extravagance of flight, its sheering off
> into delighted sky, where disappearing birds
> with feathered script will spell
> their life in flourishes
> across a naked heaven . . .
>
> as if the birds weren't there
> to animate the skies, to dive
> beneath the solid transience
> of the bridges, the joy of water
> in its rush to scatter
> their reflections, a river moving
> with its unseen weeds and fish,
> all the unstated, understood
> by context, as deer
> surmised by thickets, or plants
> missing in the moment of conjunction . . .
>
> you may live forever and not see
> a dead bird plummet down the chute
> of sky, unless you have

a hunter by your side, his rifle
with its crossed-hair sight
to catch ellipsis on the wing
and turn it to a lump of bleeding feathers
falling at the same speed as a stone
in the perfect vacuum of the sky,
an elevator falling in the mind
where gravity is just equations
and the flight of birds
is only air in hollow bones, a concept
grasped by putting out its eyes.

The sun will send the birds
like notes from silver flutes into the air;
the gun
return them in a straight line
to your feet—the perfect absence
of what is absolutely there.[6]

Wilner's vision of mathematical transcendence is demoniac where
Mona Van Duyn's was angelic: to transform a thing until it can be
correctly described by mathematical physics is to kill it. To reduce a
living animal to biochemistry one must take it apart, as a tradition
of zoological and medical experimentation has proved. Science that
can only talk about the flight of birds as a consequence of hollow
bones is linked at some fundamental level to the technology of destruction, to rifles that (for example) employ the spiral as a means for
guiding bullets more accurately to their target.

Wilner's polemic is modulated; she is far too intelligent a critic of
science to dismiss it altogether. The poem suggests obliquely that there
might be a kind of science that could cohabit with poetry. It might
see equations or geometrical curves as another way to describe,
admiringly, delightedly, the "swerving arcs" of birds in flight, one not
more authoritative than the poet's vision of them as a kind of script
that spells "their life in flourishes," like an old-fashioned hand written with a plume. Or it might study planets "in the moment of conjunction," and see their temporary obscuring as emblematic of the
mystery that makes them worthy of respect: the presence of what is

sometimes apparent, sometimes not, like deer, the depths of a river, friendship.

All the same, science contains a deadly possibility of bringing almost anything in a straight line to our feet, mastered and yet meaningless: a shapeless lump stripped of all its power of expression. If we allow our science to bring more and more of "what is absolutely there" down to "perfect absence," we will unmake ourselves. That is certainly the sibyl's warning throughout Maxine Kumin's book *Nurture*, where a poem about the struggle of Antarctic penguins for survival ends: "With zoom lenses we look in, / look in and wonder / at what flesh does for them— / we, who are going under."[7] The poem "Night Launch," subscribed "Canaveral Seashore National Park," is a poem of fear, deep-seated and monitory.

Full moon. Everyone in silhouette
graying just this side of color as we wait:
babies in Snuglis, toddlers from whose clutches
ancient blankets depend, adults encumbered
with necklaces of cameras, binoculars.
A city of people gathered on the beach.
Expectant boats jockeying offshore.

When we were kids we used to race
reciting *the seething sea ceaseth;*
thus the sea sufficeth us
and then collapse with laughter, never
having seen the rise-and-fall of ocean,
the lip of foam like seven-minute icing,
moon-pricked dots of plankton skittering.

The horizon opens, floods with daybreak,
a rosy sunrise as out of sync
as those you fly into crossing the Atlantic,
midnight behind you, the bald sky blank,
and up comes the shuttle, one costly Roman candle,
orange, silent, trailing as its rockets fall
away a complicated snake of vapor.

Along the beach a feeble cheer.
Muffled thumps of blastoff, long after,

roll like funeral drums, precise and grave.
We are the last to leave.
Driving back along the asphalt, signed
every hundred yards "Evacuation Route"
past honeycombs of concrete condominiums

I remember how we wrapped and carried
our children out to a suburban backyard
to see Sputnik cross the North Temperate Zone
at two in the morning, and how we shivered
watching that unwinking little light
move east without apparent cause.
On this warm seacoast tonight
in the false dawn my neckhairs rose.
Danger flew up to uncertain small applause.[8]

The images in this poem are those of the end of the world, though they are cast in a familiar, "suburban" idiom that makes them all the more unsettling because close to home. This is our ending: it is not biblical in scope, and no angel rises behind it, threatening and encouraging the doomed. The "city of people gathered on the beach" are only vacationing families and weekend mariners; the strange light in the sky is take-off, the funereal last trumpet take-off's boom slow as the speed of sound, and the angel a rocket ship. The remembered star in the east was only Sputnik.

The poet's response to the apparitions is an instinctive, animal reflex of terror: prickling neckhairs, shivering "without apparent cause." And the reflex is not just that of self-protection, but a fierce desire to protect her offspring: in an aside in *Nurture*'s first poem, Kumin remarks: "I suffer, the critic proclaims, / from an overabundance of maternal genes."[9] "Night Launch" is full of children: the babies and infants on the beach, the poet's child-self remembered, and the poet's children as well, when they were still small enough to be carried. The adults protect their children in Snuglis and blankets; the older children encourage themselves with security blankets and jokes, as their elders do with feeble cheers, small applause for technology's firework. But they are all in danger, and the presence of children gives the poem its tragic thrust. Some critics have claimed that children and animals can't be the subject of tragedy, only of sentimental pathos. But the suffering of children, either immediately or in its long after-math, lies at the heart of the problem of evil, and so of tragedy.

Science is not inherently evil; all human enterprises can be loaned to destructiveness, since we are so clever in our hate. Science also plays a role in human enlightenment, opening up worlds on worlds. It teaches a kind of disinterestedness and objectivity that have a moral as well as an epistemological dimension. And there is a zany, disci-plined exuberance about it, well known to the population geneticist playing upon her computer the size of a deep-freeze, and the marine biologist in hip-boots picking mussels out of the mud, and the as-tronomer following colored rosettes that blossomed a billion years ago through the small hours of the morning.

Alice Fulton, who takes novelty itself as one of her poetic topics and experiment as part of her poetic method, regularly raids science for its vocabulary and its visions. In "Cascade Experiment," the first poem in her book *Powers of Congress*, she uses the revolutionary creativity of science, that ceaselessly corrects itself and spawns new paradig-matic worlds with each revolt, as a figure for love.

> Because faith creates its verification
> and reaching you will be no harder than believing
> in a planet's caul of plasma,
> or interacting with a comet
> in its perihelion passage, no harder
> than considering what sparking of the vacuum, cosmological
> impromptu flung me here, a periphrasis, perhaps,
> for some denser, more difficult being,
> a subsidiary instance, easier to grasp
> than the span I foreshadow, of which I am a variable,
> my stance is passional toward the universe and you.
>
> Because faith in facts can help create those facts,
> the way electrons exist only when they're measured,
> or shy people stand alone at parties,
> attract no one, then go home to feel more shy,
> I begin by supposing our attrition's no quicker

than a star's, that like electrons
vanishing on one side
of a wall and appearing on the other
without leaving any holes or being
somewhere in between, the soul's decoupling
is an oscillation so inward nothing outward
as the eye can see it.
The childhood catechisms all had heaven,
an excitation of mist.
Grown, I thought a vacancy awaited me.
Now I find myself discarding and enlarging
both these views, an infidel of amplitude.

Because truths we don't suspect have a hard time
making themselves felt, as when thirteen species
of whiptail lizards composed entirely of females
stay undiscovered due to bias
against such things existing,
we have to meet the universe halfway.
Nothing will unfold for us unless we move toward what
looks to us like nothing: faith is a cascade.
The sky's high solid is anything
but, the sun going under hasn't
budged, and if death divests the self
it's the sole event in nature
that's exactly what it seems.

Because believing a thing's true
can bring about that truth,
and you might be the shy one, lizard or electron,
known only through advances
presuming your existence, let my glance be passional
toward the universe and you.[10]

One of the great virtues of science is that it allows the unexpected to
appear. And even when it forecloses on discovery because of its own
biases, its method may prompt another scientist on another day to
question those hidden presuppositions. The heroism of Galileo was
rooted in his stubborn insistence that what the eye sees, what common sense has never questioned, might be overruled. The scientists'

distrust of the senses that poets distrust so deeply also has a liberating, stimulating effect on the imagination and even on reality. Science is a device, Odyssean in its range and emphasis, that allows us "to meet the universe halfway."

Still, reality has its fault; science is not love. (But then, neither is poetry—though there is a genre called love poetry, and no love science.) Fulton holds the objective truth of science and the subjective projects of love together through that powerful instrument of poetic discovery, the analogy. Her poem-experiment is a cascade of analogies, though their verbal expression tends to suppress the obvious tags "like" and "as," presenting analogy as a species of juxtaposition. By analogy, the poet offers her analogies in the guise of scientific morphism, as if variable manifestations, electron or shy person, could be ontologically neutralized by language similar to mathematics and spoken together. But the way the poem speaks out of itself at the beginning and end, to "you," betrays its own disguise: it's a poem after all. When lovers say "I do," they bring something into existence that had not previously existed: a marriage. When a scientist measures an electron, she brings a previous existent under a new description. When a poet writes a love poem, she is more like a lover than a scientist in her creation of new facts.

All the same, the practitioners of science can show a fascination with, humility before, and devotion to its objects that are like love, very like love. Often that passionate attachment resembles the love of God rather more than love for another human being, since the objects of science in one sense constitute the cosmos and so stand in disproportion to any individual scientist. Sometimes it is a relief and a purification to be given a vanishingly small place in the big picture: science has its own catharsis. Dorothy Roberts, writing now in her ninth decade, describes this cognitive emotion in her poem "A Marvel."

> One of the images in my brain
> is a galaxy seen through a telescope years ago
> at a distance from where my life is now,
> small light blur becoming only in thought one of the great views

One of the views that can be looked at from another time
so distance lays out a plan   full of light   full of expansion
expanded back into itself and condensed
into one of the great grounds of sense

Only in thought is it realized
as more than a white breath   an enterprise in itself
where further laws are likely to be the same laws
to hold poised the great exuberance

And on and on to convert its size
into an immensity as immense   an action as intense
and governable in ways as ours
or how does it follow the heavens and yet can be recalled
to the telescope again even at this hour?

By time   years ago it was first seen
it has settled itself into the laws of dream
for the laws are the same
for inventing the telescope's eye as being in the brain
they light and relight   in inexhaustible profusion the sources of energy
a note of profoundest proportion earns them the name

More and more goes on and surrounds
the eclipsed self as the galaxy proves
in one of the great views   given of light
on the vast horizon of being
on the outskirts of all we don't have   do have and marvel at.[11]

Roberts makes clear that her seeing the galaxy "through a telescope
years ago," was incidental; her thinking the galaxy is what realizes it
in the now of the poem. Sense perception makes the galaxy small, and
blurred; thought beholds it in its true dimensions and in its au-
tonomy: "an enterprise in itself." And thought also knows the galaxy
as governed by laws, a knowledge that brings it close to the poet: for
its laws are also the laws of our own thought. The galaxy is thinkable
because it is ordered; and we can think because we participate in the
great order that eclipses but includes us. The galaxy, dream, the telescope, the brain, are held together in the "profoundest proportion"
of lawfulness.

Nor is this lawfulness the juggernaut necessity that so unsettles Nemerov, Morgan, and Wilner. It is the poise of a great exuberance, and the condition of knowing, which makes the distant near, the past present, the strange intelligible. Moments of most intense intimacy in Roberts' poetry are marked by stars: not the sentimental twinkling ones, but the ancient, distant, tremendous objects of astronomy. To her newborn grandchild, her newly dead husband, herself, she points out the stars and draws from them a consolation somewhat akin to that of Boethius or Spinoza: bereft, instructed, amazed, she insists on the truth of "one of the great views given of light."

So too Radcliffe Squires derives insight that one may call religious from his meditation on inhuman nature, putting the methodological rigor of science in the service of spiritual discipline. Scientific method requires a human being to think himself beyond the categories of experience. Practically, it is an impossible but fruitful exercise. Spiritually, it is an impossible but illuminating exercise. In poem after poem, the great desert landscapes of the American West lead Squires beyond the human to something vaster and deeper.

> The sun, they say, is dying. True, the pulse
> Of that life so pure that it kills
> Has grown debonair. But the sun's beginning
> Was only a beginning and its ending
> Will be only an end. That is the way
> Of suns—and ourselves. There is also a state
> That is neither beginning nor end, and it
> Is greater than we and greater than suns. Ponder
> These red cliffs that hang, mile after mile, in Arizona—
> I was going to say "that hang like a wave of blood
> Frozen as a warning over the mammal's world." But that's
> Not it. The cliffs are not blood. They are the harder stone,
> The harder red, that stands when the soft is gone
> Down trivial veins with the rain. Toward them,
> Rather than the sun, it seems each cactus turns,
> Discrete in its sleeve of light. And if we knew how stones
> Turn, we should see that they, too, train
> Themselves toward the cliffs. Shall we also turn

To find what is there whether sun shines
Or darkness shines, and with stones slowly feel
Ourselves becoming a body inhabiting a soul?[12]

It is quite unusual for a poet to insert a revision, a discarded revision, into the middle of a poem and make it not just a literary quirk but the hinge on which the whole poem turns. "I was going to say . . . But that's not it." Blood in our veins is blue; red blood is a symbol of life in its fatality, as blood issues from a wound. With his revision, Squires warns us away from ordinary symbolism, for he is trying to transcend human and even mammalian experience, *Urquellen* that are warm and liquid and perishable. He is not, like an ordinary mystic, trying to see past life to death, but to see past life and death taken together as the conditions of our humanity. The metaphysical secret he is after pertains as much to stones as to people, as much to darkness as the sun, for a stone or cactus can turn toward the mystery just as surely as a poet.

The evidence of all these poems, and dozens more the reader can seek out on his or her own, is that American poets do not try to ignore or escape science but resolutely, continually engage it. And the engagement produces poetry of the first rank, which succeeds meditatively as well as musically. Though the methods and aims of poetry and science are fundamentally at odds, poetry can still represent the alien mode of scientific representation in complaint and paean, polemic and riddle, caricature and hymn. The exercise certainly reveals as much about poetry as it does about science: poets test the limits of their art in such opposition and engagement. But perhaps scientists will also learn to see themselves in the mirror of poetry, and discover new possibilities in that bright, mercuric face where images pass that cannot be forgotten.

NOTES

1. *The Collected Poems of Howard Nemerov* (Chicago: University of Chicago Press, 1977), 479–80. Permission to reprint the poem was granted by Margaret Nemerov.

2. *Near Changes* (New York: Alfred A. Knopf, 1990), 67. Poem copyright 1990 by Mona Van Duyn, Alfred A. Knopf, Inc.

3. From *Near Changes*. Poem copyright 1990 by Mona Van Duyn, Alfred A. Knopf, Inc.

4. *Sigodlin: Poems* (Middletown, Conn.: Wesleyan University Press, 1990), 19. Poem copyright 1990 by Robert Morgan, Wesleyan University Press by University Press of New England.

5. Ibid., 8. Poem copyright 1990 by Robert Morgan, Wesleyan University Press by University Press of New England.

6. *Shekhinah* (Chicago: University of Chicago Press, 1984), 73–74. Permission to reprint the poem was granted by Eleanor Wilner.

7. "In Warm Rooms, Before Blue Light," from *Nurture* (New York: Viking, 1989), 5–6.

8. "Night Launch," from *Nurture*, 30–31. Poem copyright 1989 by Maxine Kumin, Penguin/Viking.

9. The title poem from *Nurture*, 3.

10. "Cascade Experiment," from *Powers of Congress* (Boston: David R. Godine, 1990), 1–2. Poem copyright 1990 by Alice Fulton. Reprinted by permission of David R. Godine, Publisher, Inc.

11. "A Marvel," from *In the Flight of Stars* (Fredericton, New Brunswick: Goose Lane Editions, 1991), 16. Roberts has published her books, and been anthologized, mostly in Canada, but she has spent her adult life in the United States and is an American citizen.

12. From *Gardens of the World* (Baton Rouge: Louisiana State University Press, 1981), 23.

Poetry and Mathematics

One of the most evocative things Paul Valéry ever said was that he wished his poems to have "the solidity of certain pages of algebra." As a poet who has been an amateur mathematician and who was for three years a teacher of advanced high school mathematics and calculus, I immediately recognize what Valéry is talking about. Passages of algebra, indented and breaking free from prose text, visually resemble passages of poetry, as if out of the plodding welter of expository prose and fastidious explanation, some higher, more intense language had suddenly burst forth like a pure aria issuing from recitative—for example, the elementary proof by "mathematical induction" that, starting with the integer 1, the sum of the first n odd integers is the square of n:

$$\sum_{p=1}^{n}(2p-1) = n^2 \Rightarrow \sum_{p=1}^{n+1}(2p-1) =$$

$$\sum_{p=1}^{n}(2p-1) + [2(n+1)-1] = n^2 + 2n + 1 = (n+1)^2.$$

When I was much younger, such flourishes of nomenclature seemed to me glamorous, abstruse, runic, and eternal, everything that, as an undergraduate poet laboring at wheezing translations from French symbolist poems, I knew that a poem should be—a hermitage of pure mind to which one could retreat from the ugly, inconvenient, and merely provisional aspects of sublunary life. Of course, all analogies limp. Mathematics cannot be a "pure aria." Of all our written languages, it is the most visual, the least oral, the language closest to silence. The first equation above, read aloud, is toneless and cumbersome, lacking the beautifully abbreviated quality of its graph: "The sum of the first p odd integers, from 1 through n, equals n squared." But the pithiness, the extreme condensation of the formula, was—still is—immensely appealing. Here was concentrated truth, applicable perhaps to many situations but, like a tiny, powerful aphoristic poem, readily possessable and portable. When I was around twenty-six, teaching calculus to five students who were smarter enough than I was to make teaching them intimidating, I tried, in a poem, to fix some of the aesthetic allure of pages of double and triple integrals:

INTEGRALS

 Erect, arched in disdain,
the integrals drift from left
across white windless pages
to the right,
serene as swans.
     Tall,
beautiful seen from afar
on the wavering water, each
curves with the balanced severity
of a fine tool weighed in the palm.

Gaining energy now, they
break into a canter—stallions
bobbing the great crests of their manes.
No one suspects their power
who has not seen them rampage.
          Like bulldozers, they build
by adding
        dirt to dirt to stumps added
        to boulders to broken glass added
        to live trees by the roots added
to hillsides, to whole
housing developments
          that roll, foaming before them,
the tumbling end of a broken wave
in one mangled sum: dandelions, old
beer-cans and broken
windows—gravestones all
rolled into one.
    Yes, with the use of tables
integration is as easy as that:
the mere squeeze of a trigger, no
second thought. The swans
cannot feel the pain
it happens so fast.

Swans, liberated from the utilitarian charts of the Chemical Rubber Company's fourteenth edition of *Standard Mathematical Tables*, like the proof sketched earlier, constitute the aspect of mathematics that Valéry, with his devotion to "poésie pure," would have especially liked. The proof is "pure" mathematics, mathematics unapplied. It is elegantly tautological: mathematical sentences that are about nothing except other mathematical sentences, just as some poems can be about poetry, which is to say, about themselves.

The raison d'être of mathematics is not, however, primarily aesthetic. Number is the most practical language that human beings have devised by which to orient themselves within the physical dimensions of the world and to measure that world. Valéry's attraction to "purity" in "pages of algebra" and in poetry is over-refined, precious. His famous analogy between poetry and dance—that poetry is to prose as dance is to walking, because poetry uses words as a dancer uses steps, as ends in themselves, whereas prose uses words as a walker uses steps, as means to an end, as mere transportation— trivializes poetry, reducing it to merely pretty language, equivalent to an entirely "pure" mathematics concerned only with elegant proofs of its own consistency. But the function of poetry, like the function of mathematics, is measurement; and "measurement" presumes that there is something to measure. What, then, does a good poem attempt to measure? And how seriously can analogies between poems and "certain pages of algebra" be drawn? Are such analogies fun but trivial? To get at answers to these questions, let us consider some of the poetry of Wallace Stevens.

Stevens was by far the most mathematically sophisticated of recent American poets. His poems regularly allude to mathematical ideas, affectionately imitate mathematical demonstrations, and apply language "mathematically" to the world. The most obviously mathematical poem of Stevens is "Anecdote of the Jar":

> I placed a jar in Tennessee.
> And round it was, upon a hill.
> It made the slovenly wilderness
> Surround that hill.
>
> The wilderness rose up to it,
> And sprawled around, no longer wild.
> The jar was round upon the ground
> And tall and of a port in air.
>
> It took dominion everywhere.
> The jar was gray and bare.
> It did not give of bird or bush,
> Like nothing else in Tennessee.

Here, the jar is the origin of a Cartesian coordinate system imposed upon the "wilderness" of a physical world unmapped in human terms.[1] Stevens is even careful to propose a vertical "z-" coordinate: the jar was "tall and of a port in air." And he is careful to remind us that the terms being imposed upon this "wilderness" are, like lines and points, wholly imaginary, wholly ideal, that this "jar" was "the only thing" in Tennessee that "did not give of bird or bush."

"Anecdote of the Jar" does not actually set out to measure anything in particular. It is about the conditions for measurement of "wilderness." Measurement is done, Stevens tells us, by imposing upon the world constructions of the imagination, ideal structures, terms that can only be sustained through something akin to Coleridge's "willing suspension of disbelief for the moment, which constitutes poetic faith." This identical phrase could be used to describe exactly the kind of assumption—the kind of "faith"—that is the basis of every mathematical construction, a construction that begins with the implicit if not the explicit injunction, "Let us assume that . . ."[2] But what does poetry, when at its best, actually measure? Stevens's "Sea Surface Full of Clouds" is a demonstration constructed expressly to address this question. The first two of the poem's five sections read as follows:

I

In that November off Tehuantepec,
The slopping of the sea grew still one night
And in the morning summer hued the deck

And made one think of rosy chocolate
And gilt umbrellas. Paradisal green
Gave suavity to the perplexed machine

Of ocean, which like limpid water lay.
Who, then, in that ambrosial latitude
Out of the light evolved the moving blooms,

Who, then, evolved the sea-blooms from the clouds
Diffusing balm in that Pacific calm?
C'était mon enfant, mon bijou, mon âme.

The sea-clouds whitened far below the calm
And moved, as blooms, in the swimming green
And in its watery radiance, while the hue

Of heaven in an antique reflection rolled
Round those flotillas. And sometimes the sea
Poured brilliant iris on the glistening blue.

In that November off Tehuantepec
The slopping of the sea grew still one night.
And breakfast jelly yellow streaked the deck

And made one think of chop-house chocolate
And sham umbrellas. And a sham-like green
Capped summer-seeming on the tense machine

Of ocean, which in sinister flatness lay.
Who, then, beheld the rising of the clouds
That strode submerged in that malevolent sheen,

Who saw the mortal massives of the blooms
Of water moving on the water-floor?
C'était mon frère du ciel, ma vie, mon or.

The gongs rang loudly as the windy booms
Hoo-hooed it in the darkened ocean-blooms.
The gongs grew still. And then blue heaven spread

Its crystalline pendentives on the sea
And the macabre of the water-glooms
In an enormous undulation fled.

In each of the five sections, certain elements of the scene—"chocolate," "umbrellas," "green," "machine," "blooms," and "clouds"—oriented with respect to "the deck"—are held as invariants in a changing light, first a "morning summer" hue, next a "streaked" "breakfast jelly yellow," next a "patterned" "pale silver," then a "mallow morning," and finally "The day . . . bowing and voluble." Each "light" projects a different atmosphere. Or, rather, each set of terms introducing the "light" determines another set of terms which, in turn, determines the distinctive ambience of each section, each "scene"— an ambience that, though believable, is conspicuously synthetic in much the same way that Eliot, in "Tradition and the Individual Talent," suggests, with his metaphor drawn from chemistry, that "art-emotion" is synthetic. When terms such as "rosy chocolate," "gilt umbrellas," "Paradisal green," "suavity," "perplexed," and "machine" are put together, they so mutually react, so color one another, that they form something new, a combination in which none of them retains its original properties: they form not a mixture but a new compound. Eliot's metaphor is more than satisfactory. It implicitly portrays the poet as a word-scientist conducting, in the laboratory of the poem, an experiment. We know, too, that behind Eliot's metaphor lies the *symboliste* enthrallment with the synthetic and with the ideal, Mallarmé's professed intent to synthesize the "flower absent from all bouquets." But if we make the short leap from a chemical metaphor to a mathematical one, we find an analogue that may be as satisfying as Eliot's; we find, in fact, that Eliot's analogy, for all its virtues, has obscured some other illuminating connections. We might think of the invariant structure of "chocolate," "umbrellas," "green," "machine," "blooms," and "clouds" as akin to coefficients in a polynomial, $f(x)$, of the form $a_n x^n + a_{n-1} x^{n-1} + \ldots + a_1 x + a_0$ in which the variable, x, the deck, can assume a different value or "light" in each section, so that each section rather playfully, as if in demonstration, yields a different value for $f(x)$ as each new "light" is substituted for x. In this poem, the "value," instead of being numerical, is aesthetic—a mood, a flavor, a feeling-tone, an intimation of something impalpable yet recognizable; for just as number is a specialized language that has evolved to express quantifiable values, poetry is the specialized language that has evolved to express synthetically otherwise inexpressible aesthetic values and experience.

We might entertain a different mathematical analogy: the "deck" in each section is analogous to the Cartesian coordinate system in two dimensions; "chocolate," "umbrellas," "green," "machine," "blooms," and "cloud" are points—the vertices of some hexagonal geometrical figure composed of vectors mapped onto the plane. This hexagonal figure seems to change in each section, as the "deck," the axes in each section, are translated or rotated or altered in scale. But actually the polygon remains invariant: only the axes with respect to which the polygon is oriented and scaled are transformed. The poem, like a mathematical demonstration, escorts us through a sequence of linear transformations. Moreover, like a mathematical demonstration, in each of its steps it succeeds, through its specialized language, in expressing "something" that, without this language, would have remained inexpressible and, because it was inexpressible, scarcely perceptible at all. It is this issue of "inexpressibility" that should enable us to appreciate fully the analogy between poetry and mathematics and how serious this analogy might be. Without mathematics, how would we describe the orbit of a planet? As "round"? As an "oval" path? How close to looking like a circle? How "eccentric"? Without the quadratic equations that graph an ellipse, we are reduced to clumsy guesses, incredibly crude linguistic approximation. The mathematical formula for the ellipse, on the other hand, can yield us the *precise* shape. It is the *only* way to express that shape. Similarly, without mathematics, how would we express the behavior of a falling object? All we could say was that it goes "faster and faster and faster." But how "fast" does it go "faster"? Only a differential equation can express this precisely and meaningfully. "Acceleration" can be measured only in mathematical terms. Indeed, the entire concept of "acceleration" is meaningful only in mathematical terms.

Is there an analogous "something" that can be expressed precisely—be measured—only by means of the specialized terms of poetry? I think so. And I think that the mysteriously impalpable moods and changes of light synthesized in each section of "Sea Surface Full of Clouds"—moods that, though seemingly ineffable, we recognize through the language of the poem—demonstrate the specialized capacity of poetic language, like mathematical language, to measure accurately and thereby to find names for areas of experience that would otherwise have eluded us. But even as I suggest this, I am poignantly aware that I cannot prove it. The poem must serve as its own demonstration. Either the reader is overcome with recognition of what had hitherto seemed insufficiently expressed, or the reader is left cold. Auden puts rather neatly this "inexpressibility" theorem of poetry, linking it with the very function of poetry itself, in the prologue to *The Sea and the Mirror*:

Well, who in his own backyard
Has not opened his heart to the smiling
Secret he cannot quote?
Which goes to show that the Bard
Was sober when he wrote.

Pope put a similar idea into somewhat more modest terms: "True wit is Nature to advantage dressed, / What oft was thought, but ne'er so well expressed." One can attempt to explicate each section of "Sea Surface Full of Clouds," to apply "interpretation" as a means of convincing the skeptical reader that there is "something" recognizable being measured and named by each section, "something" that might be mutually acknowledged with a nod or perhaps a sharp intake of breath or a bristling of the pores—by a *frisson*. But if the poem cannot accomplish this by itself—if it cannot be its own demonstration—extrinsic attempts at demonstration will never suffice, but will remain prime targets, ludicrous sitting ducks, to be coolly picked off by the poststructuralist critics. And so I will leave "Sea Surface Full of Clouds" undisturbed, trusting that it is its own sufficient testimony.

Here the analogy between poetry and mathematics is weakest. Many kinds of measurement of physical phenomena can be empirically verified at will, and each remeasurement will yield, for public verification, approximately the same numbers. The reader-response of an individual to a literary work, however, as we are often reminded in the current critical climate, can never be susceptible to such ready verification, no matter how historically, ethnically, geographically, and linguistically homogeneous the audience. Nevertheless, the entire enterprise of poetry—of literature—must operate on the assumption of commonality, of shared familiarity with literary convention. It must operate on the assumption that a reasonably sophisticated audience will derive experiences approximately congruent enough from reading the same text, that these experiences are, at least partially, communicable, and that readers of the same text can therefore use the terms of that text in order to discuss among themselves, with improved precision, their own experiences. Even "Sea Surface Full of Clouds," though seemingly untranslatable, can function this way, as well as in the private way in which Auden suggests. For example, it is easy to imagine a situation in which two people are on a cruise, the sun is rising, and one person remarks to the other, "This scene reminds me of the opening section of Stevens's 'Sea Surface Full of Clouds.' Stevens captured the mood, the light, exactly." The poem's own terms are so self-sufficient that, because they *cannot* be translated, they *need not* be. Indeed, on this very untranslatability is founded the public utility of art. Terms that first come to light in art, expressing something that had hitherto been insufficiently expressed, create their own community of those who recognize what the terms mean, what the terms refer to. The new terms then become, for that audience, a shared language that supplements and more finely differentiates the languages they had started out with. Occasionally, terms originating in works of art will pass entirely into the domain of public language, of language that does not require such specific initiation, terms, for example, like "Babbitt" and "Scrooge."

The terms in literary works are, of course, far less universally acknowledged than the truly international language of number; but both languages clearly depend upon a suspension of disbelief. This suspension of disbelief—the implicit "let us assume . . ." that makes mathematics possible—is the convention (the mathematical term might be the "axiom") that makes extrapolation possible to begin with, leading toward any number of constructions—an "algebra," a number system, a "geometry." The literary equivalent to a word like "algebra" would be the name of the genre—poetry, the novel, biography, and so on—which is the name of nothing more than a highly evolved convention. When somebody asks me, "What is a poem?" I know the answer. A poem is a convention—a highly artificial one. Although this answer usually disappoints the questioner, it implicitly describes how and even why poets write; for our sense of what a poem is and what it is for is nothing if not the sum of our memories of all the poems we have ever seriously studied or used, a list including styles as various as those of Pope and Creeley, the *Beowulf* poet and Mallarmé—what Eliot accurately characterized as The Tradition. Whenever we set out to write, we have somewhere in mind a sense of how our language should call attention to itself so as to qualify as "poetry" and to belong to the tradition—a sense rather like one that children have when, hearing "Once upon a time, . . ." they know that this opening will be followed by "there was a . . ." and that a story will unfold.

It is self-evident that conventions are never static. They are always being added onto at the margins. They evolve layer by layer, by accretions. All the layers are remembered simultaneously. Some layers fall into neglect or disrepute but may later, like the poetry of Donne, be excavated and restored to prominence, reincorporated into the most recent, hybrid, surface layer. It is during transitional periods, when a genre, poetry, is receiving a new layer or when an older, inner layer is being rediscovered, that the architects of the change will often defend their proposed alterations by trying to argue that one element or another of the convention is somehow "functional"—for example, Coleridge's defense of "metre" as providing a "medicated atmosphere" like that of "wine during animated conversation." But Coleridge's subsequent line of thought, that "every passion has its proper pulse," is closer to the truth, with its implication that poetic rhythm does not necessarily serve a function but is present as a matter of propriety. Rhythm is part of a convention adapted, Coleridge seems to be arguing, for a limited, specialized range of subject matter, one involving "passion." The word "passion" returns us directly to the question of what it is that the convention of poetry is especially adapted to measure. Is it, as Coleridge shrewdly suggests, "every passion"? Perhaps it is, though I would prefer the word "value," a concept strongly implicit in the word "passion"; for what is "passion" if not the fervent valuation of competing alternatives in some dramatic context?

We know that poems often assume other tasks than that of valuation. They tell stories. They give instructions. They flourish wit. We know, also, that other genres handle many of these tasks better than poetry. Novels are, by virtue of their length, by virtue of all the conventions of prose fiction, the most convenient format in which to portray human character and the swerving inner lives of people under the stress of changing circumstances and conflicts, in a realistically rendered historical context. Short stories are the most efficient and convenient conventional structures in which to present, replete with dialogue and details of setting, significant vignettes from people's lives. Indeed, the evolved literary genres tend to define each other's potentialities, to correct and to guide one another. One should probably not, for example, interrupt a briskly moving story to dwell on subtle moods of weather, on hints of winter light on the edges of clouds, or on the nuances and textures of a word or a phrase. Such material probably better belongs in a poem. Preaching properly belongs in sermons or in self-help manuals. We know, too, that the poem, unlike the novel or drama, has always encouraged the foregrounding of issues involving valuation, detaching such issues from the kinds of full-fledged plots and detailed human predicaments that are common and conventional in prose fiction. Moreover, because the most fundamental element of poetic convention is its display, whether through prosody, through figurative language, or through both, of a conspicuously pleasing verbal surface, at least some of the material whose value a poem attempts to measure will be language itself. It will measure the values of its own language as it goes along.

How can language measure its own value without reference to some extrinsic, critical meta-language? Through prosody, which in poetry is roughly equivalent to what formal proof is in mathematics. To fully understand how this happens, let us consider more precisely the meaning of "measurement," a word that I have been using rather cavalierly up to this point. Mathematics, the science of number, evolved as a means of measuring the physical world and for orientation within it. After "number," probably the most fundamental mathematical concept is that of ratio. Units of measure are meaningful *only* in terms of ratio. That a home run traveled five hundred feet in the air or that a basketball center is seven feet, two inches tall are facts that have meaning only in terms of our sense of what *one* foot means: that is, by comparison with some unit with which we are familiar. In other words, for a measurement, for a ratio, to alert us to its significance, it must refer to our expectations and to our remembered experiences, and it must play off of them. Of course, value that is not monetary— and particularly the value of things in themselves—cannot be framed in terms of number, and therefore it cannot, strictly speaking, be measured in terms of ratio. But if ratio is simply one form of comparison—a numerical comparison—and if, as I maintain, even in numerical comparisons ratio carries rhetorical weight only as it conspicuously accords with or violates our expectations, then we can see immediately how prosody can wring value from language itself and measure that value. To take but one example, consider how, in an accentual-syllabic prosody, the meter, because it affects every discrete syllable, foregrounds it:

> How sweet I roam'd from field to field,
> And tasted all the summer's pride,
> 'Till I the prince of love beheld,
> Who in the sunny beams did glide!

Each syllable, like a palpable nugget of paint laid on in impasto, assumes a value independent of the word in which it occurs; and by so conspicuously dividing language into units, the iambic tetrameter focuses unaccustomed attention on each unit. The "metalanguage"—the denominator implicitly weighing the numerator of Blake's language here—consists of ordinary speech and written prose. We begin to linger over the syllables in the Blake poem, to relish them by comparison to "ordinary" syllables. Suddenly, through contrast, the value inherent in the poem's language is lifted into prominence; and this contrast, though nonnumerical, is equivalent to our apprehension of ratio.

Needless to say, the beauty of good poetic language can have its source in any number of different kinds of "ratio"—so many overlapping kinds that it would be futile and pedantic to try to list, codify, or methodize them. The point of the example above is only to suggest, by illustration, a general principle: that "value" in poetry is measured and expressed by "ratio," and that the greater the organization in a poem, the more prominently will such "ratios" be thrown into relief. This same principle may hold, also, for a poem's subject matter, to the extent that "subject matter" can be considered as independent of a poem's language, as something which that language is trying to "express." Because, in good poems, structure (how "one element follows another," as Barbara Herrnstein Smith shrewdly puts it) is more highly organized over a shorter interval than in other modes of discourse, the values inherent in a poem's subject matter will, as I have suggested earlier, be thrown more prominently and more immediately into the foreground than in other modes. Value will tend to *be* the main subject matter of the poem. Indeed, it would seem to be virtually self-evident that the length of a discourse must profoundly influence how much emphasis over a given interval a given "ratio" will receive. The shorter a poem, the heavier the emphasis on any one word or sound or figure of speech. Conversely, good poems can *afford* to be shorter than, say, good short stories or novels, *because* of a poem's comparatively high density of local effects, because of the comparative frequency of the "ratios" these effects project. And this, as I have already suggested, is one of the principal ways that genres tend to define one another and to circumscribe their own areas of maximum potentiality. Indeed, even Poe's seemingly arbitrary limit of one hundred effective lines for a poem, when viewed in this light, acquires a certain plausibility.

What I have proposed, somewhat playfully, as the "inexpressibility" theorem of poetry—the notion that the very raison d'être of a poem's specialized language, like that of mathematical language, is its ability to measure, to express subject matter that, without the conventions of this language, would elude us—should not, of course, be taken too strictly. Whereas a concept such as "acceleration" is untranslatable from mathematical language, most poems are at least partially translatable, more so, at least, than Stevens's "Sea Surface Full of Clouds," which I adduced only in order to demonstrate the full implications of the analogy between poetry and mathematics when it is carried out thoroughly. Most poetry, thank heavens, is far less "pure" than what Valéry envisioned or than Stevens's "Sea Surface Full of Clouds." Pope's notion of "true wit" as "What oft was thought, but ne'er so well expressed" does not, for example, acknowledge the issue of inexpressibility. He probably means, "What oft was *said*, but ne'er so well expressed." His formulation is a pre-Romantic one. It does not acknowledge intuition. It forms a sort of lower limit for the subject matter of poetry. The range of most poetic subject matter may be located somewhere between this lower limit and Auden's "smiling secret" that we "cannot quote," the upper limit. Somewhere above this limit, presently out of bounds, might be located Mallarmé's "flower absent from all bouquets." Within these limits may be located subject matter such as we find in the following passage from Hopkins's "Binsey Poplars":

> My aspens dear, whose airy cages quelled,
> Quelled or quenched in leaves the leaping sun,
> Are felled, felled, are all felled;

Of a fresh and following folded rank
Not spared, not one
That dandled a sandalled
Shadow that swam or sank
On meadow and river and wind-wandering weed-winding bank.

In its context, the passage "That dandled a sandalled / Shadow that swam or sank / On meadow and river" constitutes what I would guess will remain the single most sufficient description in English that we will ever have of the peculiarly arresting motion of aspen leaves and their shadows in a light breeze, of the way those shadows seem to tumble and flutter as if they were underwater, the way they seem to revolve without getting anywhere, of the way the sunlight on the ground around them waxes and wanes like the light wavering on the bottom of a flowing brook, of the joyous, animate, almost playful way in which the shadows and the leaves all seem to dance together, of the way they "dandle." But already the poem's terms are tempting us back to them, away from our clumsy approximations and provisional lists. Other languages can *approximate* the true essence of aspen-leaf movement, but they cannot measure it as precisely as this poem's language can; nor can they exactly translate this poem's language, which remains the single perfect formula not only for the inscape of those lost trees but for all the aspens that I can remember and—because poetic language as fully realized as Hopkins's bequeaths us formulas so powerful as to be nearly universal—the rest of the aspens I will ever see and sit under and relish redundantly.

NOTES

1. Is it an accident or characteristic of Stevens's wit and attention to minutiae that the round mouth of the jar just happens to resemble the zero at the origin of a Cartesian coordinate system and the letter "o" of "origin"?

2. In Stevens's "Connoisseur of Chaos" the passage "The pensive man . . . He sees that eagle float / For which the intricate Alps are a single nest" alludes to the suspension of disbelief that allows us to view a line as both one continuum ("single nest") and as a set of discrete points (the separate peaks of "Alps").

STEPHANIE STRICKLAND

Seven-League Boots

Poetry, Science, and Hypertext

The highest order of the imaginative intellect is always pre-eminently mathematical; and the converse.—Edgar Allan Poe

[1] I want to speak to you about a hypertext poetics.

[2] In a hypertext, any part can link to any other, or be unlinked, or re-linked, at any time. Hypertexts live on computers. There is never only one way to read them.

[3] The world's biggest hypertext is the Internet. Let me tell you a story. Once upon a time, a powerful Soviet space physicist, who had defected from his country, with wife and daughter, in order to come to Princeton to develop the physics of quantum gravity, quit. Gone was his goal of building a theory integrating all the forces in nature, knocked out of his head by the World Wide Web. Sasha Migdal began,

instead, to write software that makes lifelike models of people because, he said, "I had dreamed since I was a child of a giant network connecting everybody like a single brain. Of course, it's not true yet. But there is a real revolution going on, and I just couldn't resist it."

[4] On the Web, to point is to ride Aladdin's carpet, or to stride with seven-league boots. It's a strange way of traveling, outside of fairy tales. Time zones and geographies collapse; but oddly enough, people online feel both in touch and in control, for they move by their own choice in a field of many choices. Poetry and science share three aspects of hypertext—the conviction that any part can link to any other, and should; that it is appropriate to live in an environment that spans space and time; that it is desirable to be both closely in touch and in control.

[5] Simone Weil, the French philosopher and mystic, proposed that all art and science should reflect our idea of ultimate value. For her, the behavior most appropriate to moral life is what she called "attention," an act of letting judgment fall away and bringing oneself again and again to fresh encounter with the world. She said, "A fixed point of view is the root of injustice," a dictum that shows an appreciation for the re-seeing required by hypertext.

[6] Simone Weil distinguished different ages in the history of science according to the values they embodied. She claimed that Greek science was motivated by ideals of "balance" and "beauty." The Greeks, she said, saw a moving waterline on a hull as an image of balance; whereas Newton, in the next age of science, one that valued energy and work, saw a loaded-down ship, saw force and displacement.

[7] Born in 1913, the poet Muriel Rukeyser took the science of Edison and the Wright Brothers as a tool for her work. Her first book of poems, *Theory of Flight*, was named for her aviation manual. Working as a journalist and film editor, Rukeyser brought new proto-hypertextual techniques to her writing, creating a swappable stream of scenes on which she imposed cuts, to make associative links.

[8] Rukeyser identified America, as did Whitman, with its diversity; she was certain no part must be excluded. In her second book, *U. S. 1*, she investigated the fatal silicosis afflicting miners in West Virginia. The revolutionary achievement of this book was to create a poem as database, using materials never before seen in poetry—stock-market quotes, doctors' reports, and legal testimony, side by side with lyric and narrative. This database, this hypertextual organization, makes an implicit claim; namely, that the fullest range of textual type is required to understand and combat injustice.

[9] Pulling together yet other worlds she felt had been artificially separated, Rukeyser wrote the biography of the mathematical physicist Willard Gibbs. Gibbs, in the nineteenth century, devised visualizing methods that redefined the meaning of space. Instead of being a static Cartesian grid, his phase space could represent every possible lifeline of a system, any system, any number of coexisting systems. Gibbs's method, criticized by some as *merely* visualizing, was grasped at once by James Clerk Maxwell—the man whose equations define electronic reality—as both profound and productive. The very shapes of graphs and models yielded truths about energetics of the system— the relation of transitions to degrees of freedom and free energy; phase transition itself, as from ice to water, being a change of identity toward which the whole system was attracted.

[10] William Blake also used "visualizing" methods. His poems, made from the interaction of full-scale drawings, patterns intertwined with text, and calligraphic gestures, could not be interpreted by conventions developed to understand print. Blake's work demanded a new poetics of "in-betweenness" in order to understand the relation of text, image, graphic gesture, and pictorial convention. Reading "between"—reading the link, or gap—remains a provocation and pleasure of fully developed hypertext.

[11] Emily Dickinson also refused to commit her work to print convention. She refused to title more than 1,700 poems, and she evolved singular methods of both production and punctuation. But her most

radical innovation, extraordinary still, was the hyperlink experience she provided in many of her poems. She placed a superscript cross (as we would place a footnote marker) to indicate words, or places, where she wished the reader to consider a range of choices. The choices she wanted to present were inscribed across the bottom of her page. These crosses—or crossroads-markers—are not signs of preliminary indecision; they are, carefully copied on pages that are carefully sewn together, endorsements of multiple meaning.

[12] Simone Weil died in England in 1943. What word might she have chosen, had she lived, to name value for us, as "balance" and "beauty" named value for the Greeks? I would propose her Greek term μεταξυ, translated as "resonant communication." Resonance entails response, interaction, co-creation, a space between.

[13] Quantum reality, the reality of electronic computers, works by resonance. It is hard to overstate how deeply our lives are shot through with computation. Computers are not a tool we use; it is closer to the truth to say that computes are every tool we use: our watches, cars, credit cards, libraries, phones. . . . Insofar as the computer is our tool, we are electronically animate—but what does it mean to be an avatar, cyborg, or animation? Questions of identity, location, change, and closure become acute.

[14] How will the readers and writers of multiply linked text, of hypertext, know who they are or how to trust each other, when comprehensive knowledge eludes them both? How can we build resonant communication—how stay in touch, but also in control, in the face of what easily overwhelms us?

[15] We are overwhelmed, not only by the proliferation of paths that hypertext provides, but by an explosion of data. Data has gotten beyond human ability to process it unaided. The amount and kind of data is now so vast that negotiations need to be made with computers to read it, for they alone can handle the load. NASA collects a trillion bytes of data a day, just from satellites. The self-documenting

form our lives take, as we conduct them electronically, every keystroke captured, also leaves data shadows in our wake. Does such data represent our capture by alien, that is, humanly unreadable, information, or can it be understood as a solicitation of "attention," in Simone Weil's sense?

[16] What we "see," what we get from our electronic devices, are numbers. The decisions we make, in order to bring numbers into full "living" color, contain many suppositions and are often aesthetic. If we are living in virtual worlds, it is because we live in worlds furnished with complex visualizations, be these composited news photos, or *Toy Story*—the first computer-generated film—or Rover on Mars, or holographs, or the Cosmic Voyage IMAX feature that shows the first few seconds of the universe. These late-twentieth-century ways of seeing, of knowing, are easily misunderstood, mystifying on their grand scale. What they most lack is words—the words of poets, or other representatives of the lone human voice, of the great value to be placed on each lone human voice.

[17] The task today, in both poetry and science, is the measure of measure. Which numbers, from an only partially searchable store, will we translate, or render, calling them truths? What colors will we give them to bring them "alive," knowing what we know of the ease with which people are persuaded to cruelty? A poetics of hypertext should answer this question: how to become as resonant and co-participatory as the quantum world is.

EDITOR'S NOTE

To experience this essay in hypertext form, as it was first published in the *Electronic Book Review*, Issue 7 (summer 1998), go to http://altx.com/ebr/ebr7/7strick/

ALICE FULTON

Fractal Amplifications

Writing in Three Dimensions

During the last quarter of the twentieth century, science turned away from regular and smooth systems in order to investigate more chaotic phenomena. Rather than being divided into the classical binaries of order and entropy, form now can be regarded as a continuum expressing varying degrees of the pattern and repetition that signal structure. As architect Nigel Reading writes, "Pure Newtonian causality is an incorrect (finite) view, but then again, so is the aspect of complete uncertainty and (infinite) chance." The nature of reality now is "somewhere . . . between."[1] It occurs to me that this shift in focus makes itself felt within literature as postmodernism. In any case, the poetry I am calling "fractal" shares many defining traits of that contested term: postmodern. Since other contemporary poetries show a greater allegiance to Romantic, confessional, or formalist traditions, fractal aesthetics describe—or predict, if you will—only one feature of the topography. I say "predict" because I hope these remarks will suggest future vistas. When poets address aesthetics, their own work inevitably shades their views. I write from perceptions of where my poems have lately been and where they're likely headed.

Earlier drafts of this essay included a few exemplary poems by contemporaries, but these specific instances became points of contention as readers argued with my choices and proposed their own. Perhaps this was inevitable: the short poems suitable for inclusion in an essay cannot illuminate the maximalist aesthetic I describe. And since I am proposing a largely untried poetics, a poetics more emergent than existent, few examples are available.[2] I hope readers will imagine or build, identify or locate, the representative works themselves. Before declaring a poem "fractal," I suggest that you ask whether comic, bawdy, banal, or vulgar lines are spliced to lyrical, elegiac, or gorgeous passages. Ask whether resistant (dense) surfaces are juxtaposed with transparent (lucid) areas. Those features seem fundamental. They offer an obvious place to begin.

In the 1970s, the mathematician Benoit Mandelbrot found that certain structures once thought to be "chaotic" contained a deep logic or pattern. The communication between roots and leaves; the oscillations of cotton futures; the movement of spiraling funnel galaxies; the branching of arteries and veins; and the curved, nonlinear structure of space-time itself are examples of chaotic phenomena found to contain fractal designs. Mandelbrot coined the word "fractals" (from the Latin *fractus*, meaning "irregular or fragmented") to describe such configurations.[3] In my 1986 essay, "Of Formal, Free, and Fractal Verse: Singing the Body Eclectic," I suggested that science's insights concerning turbulence might help us to describe traits common to the poetry of volatile (rather than fixed) form. I proposed that we view the irregular yet beautifully structured forms of nature as analogues and call the poetry of irregular form *fractal verse*.[4]

Just as fractal science analyzed the ground between chaos and Euclidean order, fractal poetics could explore the field between gibberish and traditional forms. It could describe and make visible a third space: the nonbinary *in-between*. Consider water. At low temperatures, it is fully ordered in the form of ice; at higher temperatures it becomes fluid and will not retain its shape. The stage between ice (order) and liquid (chaos) is called the transition temperature. Fractal poetics is interested in that point of metamorphosis, when structure is incipient, all threshold, a neither-nor. Over the past decade, scientists have come to view fractals as particular instances within the larger field of complexity theory. While retaining the term "fractal poetry," I hope to suggest ways in which complexity theory might amplify the possibilities of such a poetics. (A poem is not a complex adaptive system: the comparison is analogical, not literal.)

My tentative 1986 prospectus for postmodern fractal poetry suggested that digression, interruption, fragmentation, and lack of continuity be regarded as formal functions rather than lapses into formlessness and that all shifts of rhythm be equally probable. Of course, disjunction also informed high-modernist aesthetics. Postmodernism seems more an elaboration of that tradition than a wholly new formation. The new always contains aspects of the old: novation springs from the existent. Hand-me-downs are recombined and during the process freshness (a strange entity that might seem wrong or counterintuitive at first) seeps in. Perhaps it's nothing new to say that newness is a composite. Rather than elide this truism, however, postmodernism rejects originality and stresses the inevitability of appropriation in creative work. The prefix "post" signals a foundational debt and an unabashedly reactive position that departs from a modernist make-it-new credo.

Common sense, moreover, suggests that contemporary work must be inflected by the pressures of its day regardless of the poet's willed intentions. Even a strenuous attempt to duplicate a previous aesthetic would fall into the temporal gap and become, at best, ventriloquism. Difference is a given. Describing that shift—the changes in poetry's metabolism across generations and time—is an ongoing project for scholars and poets. Recent scholarship has suggested alternative modernisms that enlarge the view. In this essay, however, Pound's well-known "A Few Don'ts by an Imagiste"[5] and "The Waste Land"[6] will serve as high-profile reference points. Pound and Eliot, more than any other literary figures, defined literary modernism during the twentieth century. Pound's directives were the catechism of poetry workshops during the sixties and seventies. As a result, his precepts possibly have exerted a greater effect on contemporary poetry than they did on the poetry of his own day.

In *Hidden Order*, John H. Holland writes that complex systems possess "a dynamism" that is different from the static structure of a computer chip or snowflake, which are merely complicated.[7] Complex systems are balanced on the edge of chaos, where the components "never quite lock in place, and yet never quite dissolve into turbulence either."[8] A rain forest, the immune system, the economy, and a developing embryo are examples of complex adaptive systems. In poetics, Holland's "dynamism" makes itself felt in eccentric forms that share broad similarities, in contrast to more "static" received forms with specific similarities. This essay describes those broadly similar traits and calls the poetry that shares them "fractal." Lest my descriptions seem to imply otherwise, I must assert that aesthetics are not a progress narrative: it isn't getting better all the time. It's getting different all the time.

On the ground between set forms and aimlessness a poem can be spontaneous and adaptive—free to think on its feet rather than fulfill a predetermined scheme. In a departure from Romantic ideals, fractal aesthetics suppose that "spontaneous" effects can be achieved through calculated as well as *ad libitum* means. Thus, "spontaneity" does not refer to a method of composition, but to linguistic gestures that feel improvisatory to the reader. Riffing and jamming, rough edge and raw silk—such wet-paint effects take the form of long asides, discursive meanderings, and sudden shifts in diction or tone. By such means "spontaneity" becomes a structural component of the poem.

Complex adaptive systems do not seek equilibrium or try to establish balance; they exist in unfolding and "never get there." As Holland says, "the space of possibilities is too vast; they have no practical way of finding the optimum."[9] Like complex systems, fractal poetry exists within a vast array of potentialities: it is a maximalist aesthetic. High modernism also was much of a muchness. At 433 lines, "The

Waste Land" may not be a long poem by today's standards, but it is long when compared with the imagist poems of its time. Perhaps *The Cantos*, at roughly 23,000 lines, offers the best prefiguration of contemporary maximalism. In any case, the high-modernist impulse toward length seems different in kind from the spirit informing today's long poem.

For at least part of his career, Pound espoused a modernist renaissance that would draw on the example of rightly governed past cultures. His aesthetics were imbued with his sense of historicity, a backward gaze that became increasingly elegiac as his discouragement gained force. Modernist maximalism, as practiced by Pound and Eliot, was a structure of depletion: the poem spent itself as a gesture of mourning—for lost civilizations and mythologies. Its exhaustion was nihilistic in spirit, much ado about nothing ("I can connect / Nothing with nothing,"[10] ". . . emptiness is the beginning of all things"[11]). To risk a generalization, their modernism beautifully encountered what-is-not and gave ample voice to absence. The postmodern poem, on the other hand, is an architecture of excess; it spends itself by reveling in the plethora of what-is. Its exhaustion is celebratory—or hedonistic, grasping. With the A-bomb's ashes for its grim confetti, it means to *carpe diem* all night long, whistling in the dark context of impending (rather than ended) apocalypse. Built from presence, it has a life-wish. Taken together, the two modernisms resemble a twentieth-century lost and found.

Although a fractal poem might offer transcendence at the local level— in a line, a phrase—like a complex adaptive system it does not try to sustain a sublime optimum throughout. Its high-lyric passages might be juxtaposed with vulgar or parodic sections; its diction can range from gorgeous to caustic. These oscillations occur with no change of speaker since fractal poetics is not a voice-based aesthetic. Williams's variable foot arose from his observation that "the iamb is not the normal measure of American speech."[12] And Pound stipulated that poetry's language must "depart in no way from speech save by a heightened intensity (i.e., simplicity)." Poetry must contain "nothing that you couldn't, in some circumstance, in the stress of some emotion, actually say. Every literaryism, every book word, fritters away a scrap of the reader's patience, a scrap of his sense of your sincerity."[13] (Of course, Pound did not take his own advice. But hundreds of poets did—and do.) "Naturally," he wrote, "your rhythmic structure should not destroy the shape of your words, or their natural sound, or their meaning."[14]

Fractal poetics has dispensed with fidelity to the "normal" and the "natural," to "simplicity" and "sincerity." Instead of reproducing speech, the poem makes a sound-unto-itself; its music is not so much voiced as built. Even the most "sincere" or "natural" poem is a means, however unwitting or disavowed, of manipulating the reader. Fractal verse heightens the distinction between art and life rather than creating an insincere sincerity. Marjorie Perloff describes it splendidly: "Whereas Modernist poetics was overwhelmingly committed, at least in theory, to the 'natural look,' . . . we are now witnessing a return to *artifice* but a 'radical artifice,' to use Lanham's phrase, characterized by its opposition, not only to 'the language really spoken by men' but also to what is loosely called Formalist (whether old or new) verse, with its elaborate poetic diction and self-conscious return to 'established' forms and genres. Artifice, in this sense, is less a matter of . . . elaboration and elegant subterfuge, than of the recognition that a poem . . . is a *made thing*—contrived, constructed, chosen."[15]

Fractal form might counter such "natural" effects as breaking lines on nouns and verbs; it might favor music that unhinges rather than reinforces the poem's content. Such effects call attention to themselves, and in doing so they highlight the "radical artifice" that is the poem's surface and disrupt its transparency. Diction, surface textures, irregular meters, shifts of genre, and tonal variations take center stage as defining formal elements. Function words (articles, conjunctions, prepositions) assume schematic importance. The content of fractal poetry's form (yes, the *content* of *form*) also dismantles assumptions concerning "the natural." Form's subversive or reactionary possibilities are recognized rather than denied.

Holland's *Hidden Order* notes that when reading formal structures we decide to call some aspects irrelevant; we agree to ignore them. "This has the effect of collecting into a category things that differ only in the abandoned details."[16] The form of Petrarchan sonnets, for instance, differs only in those structural aspects we choose to overlook. We focus on the identical rhyme scheme, the iambic pentameter, the "turn" at line nine. We examine properties that define the sonnet and disregard properties that fall outside of this definition. Fractal poetics is composed of the disenfranchised details, the dark matter of Tradition: its blind spots, recondite spaces, and recursive fields.

When structure is imbued with substance, when form carries freight, the poem need not resort to polemical narrative or didactic anecdote as a means of airing its engagements. Its "political" explorations, structurally embedded, can retain subtlety. The gender of pronouns and the relation of linguistic figure and ground can provide a formal means of addressing cultural visibility and negation. Punctuation, rather than effacing itself, can become a glyph of implication (as the leveling, democratic colon does in the poetry of A. R. Ammons, for instance).

The emphasis on ground rather than figure necessarily changes the poem's point of view. If "The Waste Land" were written from the perspective of the woman who says "My nerves are bad to-night," the resultant work might resemble Rich's "Snapshots of a Daughter-in-Law." "You! hypocrite lecteur!—mon semblable,—mon frère!" Eliot quotes from the preface to *Fleurs du Mal*.[17] "The argument, *ad feminam*, all the old knives / that have rusted in my back, I drive in yours, / *ma semblable, ma sœur!*" Rich revises.[18] Rather than conversing with "The Waste Land," it seems to me that Rich enacts a radical reversal of ground by placing one of Eliot's peripheral "voices" at the center of her poem.

There are two kinds of fractals: geometric and random. The geometric type, by repeating an identical pattern at various scales, suggests new dimensions of figure and ground. The fractal's smaller parts replicate the form of the entire structure, turned around or tilted a bit, and increasing detail is revealed with increasing magnification. My long sequence, "Give," can be seen as a fractal reimagining of the Daphne and Apollo legend from Ovid's *Metamorphoses*. In my telling, the story changes scale; the myth is blown-up: enlarged and exploded. Daphne, who was voiceless in Ovid, is given words. And after she is turned into a tree, the subjugated, silent laurel speaks—literally speaks—to the human intrusion into nature. Ovid's bit players—victimized Daphne and the violated tree—are magnified and given starring roles.[19]

To say that the politics of masculinist high modernism were different from those in the previous paragraphs is to understate. Rather than culturally inflected icons and scripts, Eliot and Pound viewed archetypes and mythology as revelations of "essential drives": universal, *natural* truths whose meanings apply across time and place. They identified the loss of such mythology with spiritual bankruptcy. The feminist postmodern poem, on the other hand, seeks to discredit the pandemic power of myth. It questions the assumption of "naturalness" surrounding, for instance, heterosexuality, human sway over animals and planet, woman's association with nature and man's with culture. The loss of such "natural" truths is seen as a potential source of spiritual gain.

Of course, postmodern aesthetics do not automatically assume "high" art to be more interesting than "low." I find the engagement with popular culture to be somewhat troublesome and contradictory, however. Attention is a form of homage. And our fascination as a culture fed upon commercial art throughout the twentieth century. "Serious," "composed," contemporary music, for instance, has been neglected to such a degree that we lack an adjective to describe it. Throwing euphemism to the winds, I refer to it as *un*popular music. Such music is less commodified, clearly, than popular genres. It also is of high quality and deserving of more notice. If fractal poetics means to honor the margins and illuminate the fringes—the quirky handmade rather than slickly mass-produced, the bit players and backdrop rather than the spectacles and principals—*un*popular art, though redolent of "high" culture, must be part of its subject. The example of music extends to the visual arts and to literature. Whatever is complex and underinvestigated must become the starring subject.

And yet, the implications of popular culture—and the engines of its power—have come under scrutiny only recently. Rather than exclude the popular, fractal aesthetics want to understand its magnetism—and sometimes richness. "Consider the way of the scientist rather than the way of the ad agent," Pound advised.[20] Fractal poetics considers both. Neither elitist nor populist, it exists on a third ground between "high" and "low" terrain, resistant to those classifications. Like the components of complex systems, the poems' inclusions neither lock into position nor dissolve into turbulence.

The structure of complex adaptive systems is determined by internal models. In like fashion, the fractal poem's growth and resolution are activated by self-determined imperatives rather than by adherence to a traditional scheme. But how does the inner imperative of fractal verse differ from the organic form of free verse? In 1918, Pound stated the organic credo as succinctly as his Romantic predecessors or the Black Mountain poets who succeeded him: "I believe in an 'absolute rhythm,' a rhythm, that is, in poetry which corresponds exactly to the emotion or shade of emotion to be expressed."[21]

Though modernism has come to be associated with discontinuity, Pound seemed to regard "The Waste Land" as a model of cohesive design. In a letter of praise to Eliot he admonished himself for "never getting an outline" in his own poems.[22] For me, the wholeness of "The Waste Land" arises from its singleness of tone and symbolic coherence. Its polyphonic voices wear a gray membrane of irony; the sensibility throughout is measured and austere. There are no petards. Nothing funny or vulnerable is to be found in its shifting lines. Eliot's rhetoric never veers into confession or exposition. Fractal poetry, on the other hand, splices satiric and lyrical, elegiac and absurd lines without casting a unifying tonal veil over the mélange. But the distance between the mod and the post- is nowhere more evident than in their respective stands toward the symbolic. Contemporary poetry prefers metaphoric to symbolic encodings. A poem as self-consciously and determinedly allusive as "The Waste Land" would seem old-fashioned if written today; the water/desert trope, heavy-handed and shopworn.

Modernist discontinuity tended to be grounded in mimesis and realism. Its disjunctions sought to replicate the mechanistic quality of urban life and the beginning of the age of information (as figured by telephone, film, and radio). Rather than mirroring its age, fractal disruption functions as a Zen slap, awakening readers from the spell of the "sincere" voice. It contrasts transparent lines with less "genuine" dictions, and the disparate tones vibrate like complementary colors, highlighted by proximity. The poem thrums with bone-conduction music as registers vibrate in concert with unlikenesses spliced nearby.

Both organic and fractal form compare poetry to structures in the natural world. Organic form, however, extends this prizing of nature to imitations of the "natural" speaking voice. Fractal poetry, as we have seen, regards voice as a construct: a consciously made assemblage of dictions, meters, rhetorics, gestures, and tones. Whereas organicism insists upon wholeness and smoothness of thought, fractal poetry regards interruption, artifice, disjunction, and raggedness as facets of its formal vocabulary. In practice, these differences mean that the textures of fractal poetry will be more turbulent than those of organic free verse. A fractal poem might establish iambic pentameter only to break it with rudely dissonant effects. It locates structure in disruption and allows new (or old) forms to emerge as the poem proceeds.

Organic aesthetics, by definition, try to match the poem's cadence with its emotional content. Feelings must be expressed in a "natural" speaking voice, lest they sound stilted or become inaccessible. If the verse is truly organic (and in *The Cantos* it is not) its language will vanish into meaning when read rather than linger opaquely on the page as an indecorous reminder that poems are made of words. Fractal aesthetics, in contrast, refract the poem's surface in order to make its linguistic materiality more evident. As free verse broke the pentameter, fractal verse breaks the poem plane.

The poem plane is analogous to the picture plane in painting: a two-dimensional surface that can convey the illusion of spatial depth. Painters use perspective, colors, texture, and modeling to suggest three dimensions on the flat canvas. If objects are painted progressively smaller and closer together they will seem to recede. Space also can be suggested by juxtaposing oncoming warm colors with introverted cool ones. By alternating thickly textured impasto with turpentine-thinned washes, the artist can create opaque areas of positive space and radiant glazes of negative space. Objects of the same scale can be modeled differently to create depth: a hard-edged rendering will appear nearer than a hazy one.

A composition's rhythm sometimes depends on repeating picture planes through multiple zones of recession until the painting gives credence to spaces ungoverned by the laws of physics. In Poussin's *The Funeral of Phocion*, for instance, the picture plane is repeated as walls, buildings, and hills recede toward the final backdrop of sky. John Canaday describes the effect this way: "A second series of planes at an angle to the picture plane is suggested first by the side plane of the stone wall at the right. We enter the picture from the lower left corner and move across it, but are kept from moving out by the tall tree at the right and by this plane of the wall, which is turned to deflect the 'current' of our movement back into the picture. It is not noticeable that this plane is, in fact, a distortion of true perspective."[23]

The eye moves from left to right across the painting until a tree and a plane of wall at the far right rebound the gaze back into the picture. In poetry, a justified flush-right margin (instead of the usual flush-left alignment) will halt the eye abruptly, almost rudely, stranding the gaze in an unbidden white surround before deflecting it leftward and into the next line. Such a "distortion" underscores the poem's constructedness; it also offers a subtle formal means of reinforcing content.

The motion of reading is horizontal and vertical: our eyes skim across and edge down the flat planes of print. Poetry has held language to this single plane rather than using linguistic properties as a means of constructing three-dimensional space. "To be fractal a form must be . . . between dimensions," notes Nigel Reading.[24] Just as paint fosters illusions of proximity and distance on canvas, words can suggest spatial depth on paper. A fractal poem can do this by shifting its linguistic densities: The poem's transparent, "easy" passages impart the sensation of negative space; they vanish into meaning when read rather than calling attention to their linguistic presence. More textured language, on the other hand, refuses to yield its mass immediately. The eye rests on top of the words, trying to gain access, but is continually rebuffed. Such (relatively) opaque sections assume the solidity of positive space. By juxtaposing transparent with textured passages, fractal poetry constructs a linguistic screen that alternatively dissolves and clouds.

Planes of varying densities move us into and out of the poem, as if it were a field of three dimensions. We gaze "through" thin lines and are deflected to the surface by "showier," distracting, dense language. This modulating depth of field allows us to experience the poem as a construct of varying focal lengths. Such palpable architectonics also create an awareness of the poem as thing-in-itself rather than con-duit for meaning. I've used the words "transparent" and "textured" to describe two broad effects. Perhaps it's worth noting that transpar-ent lines are not drawn solely from simple, lyric registers. They also can be forged of exposition, reportage, platitudes, advertisements, or clichés. What they have in common is lucidity. And textured passages are not composed only of arcane, difficult words. Density need not be leaden or dull. "Texture" can be built, for instance, from sequined, wooly, stippled, flannel, marbled, glittery, or drippy linguistic regis-ters. Resistance is key.

What I'm suggesting is that poetry take advantage of a synesthesia that attributes physicality (color and texture) to language. For me, and I think for many linguistically addicted people, words have an unignorable materiality. It is not only the meaning of words that holds my attention, but their sensual, and especially tactile, presence. Pas-sages can have an ultrasuede nap, like the velour finish of a petal, or they can feel prickly as hairbrushes. I am bored by poetry constructed solely of thin, homogenous tones because it reads like a field of gray plaster. I think most readers possess some degree of synesthesia. Fractal verse develops this ability to feel language as a 3-D tactile sur-round. Perhaps its greatest urgency exists in its potential for limbic awakening.

Of course, *The Cantos* also can be read as "planes in relation." Yet that staggering poem does not create a sense of three-dimensional space; it splices disparate people and places so that readers can draw inferences from the allusive montage. Pound modeled his poem plane on the ideogram or concrete picture, and *The Cantos* strives for a uniform degree of concretion rather than a plate tectonics of transparent and textured passages. "Don't use ... 'dim lands of peace,'" he famously advised. "It dulls the image. It mixes an abstraction with the concrete. It comes from the writer's not realizing that the natural object is always the *adequate* symbol."[25] Pound's later practice—in which the "natural object" became a preexistent text spliced into the poem—was more complex than his early theory would lead one to suppose. Poetry-writing textbooks and workshops over the past thirty years have taken his injunction to "go in fear of abstraction" at face value, nonetheless. In the grammar school of imagism, contemporary poets learn that "dim lands" imply "peace." This might be a useful place to begin, but it's a facile place to end up.

Rather than excise stale portmanteaus, fractal poetry might use empty rhetoric sardonically, as a means of splintering the "sincere" voice that was a modernist value. Abstractions are arguably the most rarified words because they have no relation to a specific physical object. In fractal poetics, abstractions are not foresworn as redundant explications of self-sufficient concrete symbols; rather the abstract becomes a valuable realm in itself, a means of adding ether, gassiness, fumes, breath to the poem's corporate mix. By adjoining abstract with concrete pigments, poets are afforded another method of refracting the poem plane.

As soon as one begins to analyze or dissect a poem's formal components, the poem is no longer organic or "whole." This is why organicism seems the antithesis of formalism. And it explains why organic free verse never developed a vocabulary with which to describe its formal properties. Although fractal poetry does not adhere to a predetermined scheme, it offers a terminology (planes, surface, canopy, textures, transparency, opacity, obverse, metabolism, understory, cluster, supercluster, limbic ...) that is descriptive of its structure. The vocabulary used to describe form changes the way that we think of form. And changes in thinking emerge as changes in the work.

The New Critics believed poems rended by formal analysis were reconstituted within the readers' improved understanding. Rather than stressing the retrievable wholeness of separate parts, fractal poetics investigate—and prize—the spaces between the parts. In *Chaos: Making a New Science*, James Gleick writes, "One simple but powerful consequence of the fractal geometry of surfaces is that surfaces in contact do not touch everywhere. The bumpiness at all scales prevents that.... It is why two pieces of a broken teacup can never be rejoined, even though they appear to fit together at some gross scale. At a smaller scale, irregular bumps are failing to coincide."[26] The excerpt hints at concepts dear to fractal aesthetics: surfaces, touch, bumpiness, scale, broken, irregular, and failing.

Failing might seem an unlucky inclusion, but with it I mean to suggest not only a relinquishment of subter*fusion* but a taste for subterfuge in the guise of accidents, pratfalls, slippage, and mistakes. I have two copies of "The Waste Land." One is a recent, clean edition. The other, the one I favor, is a used paperback remastered by the marginal scribbling of some eager, previous reader. One comment refers to "the lonely, arid *dessert* within," and the phrase's connotations are more interesting than the "right" words would have been. Fractal poetry is enthralled by such failures and fallshorts, such improving accidents. "Plan addiction with Hank," I find on a to-do list. And in a letter, "I'll have it to you by the end of the month." Lengthy, scholarly notes at the end of poems (as in "The Waste Land" or Marianne Moore's books) predate this sense of the absurd. Unless such notes become creative works in themselves (a parodic means of undoing the poem's precious gestures, for instance), they remain a mod trait.

Marjorie Perloff noted that the poetry of "radical artifice" is not to be confused with formalist verse, which depends on established forms and genres and whose artifice is based on elaboration and elegance. I would add that poetry in received forms can be likened to standard mathematics (calculus, say, or linear analysis) in which the value of the parts adds up to the value of the whole. That is, the strength of a metered poem's lines adds up to the poem's strength as a whole. The disjunctive shifts of fractal poetry, however, are akin to nonlinear interactions in which the value of the whole cannot be predicted by summing the strength of its parts. A fractal poem might contain purposely insipid or flowery lines that would be throwaways if taken out of context. When juxtaposed with other inclusions, however, these debased lines establish a friction or frame greater than their discrete presence would predict.

Complex systems tend to recycle their components. A rain forest, for instance, captures and reuses critical resources as a means of enriching itself. Fractal poetry likewise makes use of recurring cluster words, limbic lines, or canopy stanzas as a means of creating depth. (*Cluster* being an aggregation of stars with common properties; *limbic* connoting emotion and motivation; *canopy* casting a shade overall.) Unlike the villanelle or sestina's recycling, fractal repetition does not appear at a predetermined place within a set scheme. The poem is more dynamic and turbulent because its repetitions have an element of ambush. Readers experience the consolation of pattern without being able to anticipate the moment of return. Such recycling, at once surprising and reassuring, can occur throughout a poem, book, or body of work. (Dickinson's recurring vocabulary comes to mind.)

Skeptical readers might think *Dickinson? What is she doing here?* And *Poets have always used repetition.* I can only say again that newness is a composite. Dickinson—with her broken syntax and maximal dashes—is a fractal forbearer. And though all structures rely on repetition, poets have not used recycling in conjunction with the other effects I've described. Novation also is created by context and label: free verse was written before the modernists popularized the term, yet twentieth-century unrhymed poetries of variable meter sound like none other.

Though this might be the maximalist talking, I sense there is much more to say. My intent here has been more visionary than critical: that is, I've described an incipient poetics, one that I feel forming as I write and read. I've taken the liberty of devising a vocabulary as necessary. I've looked toward unmet horizons rather than existing territories. Generalizations must be customized to particular poets since each turns on her own axis. Each builds her emancipations by hand. That such freedoms can speak to one another is my fair calculation: that difference can be tempered by affinity. I leave the compass of that conversation to you.

NOTES

1. Nigel Reading, "Dynamical Symmetries: Autopoietic Architecture," 20 August 1998, http://www.giant.co.uk/phimega.html.

2. For examples of fractal aesthetics in action, read *The Snow Poems* (New York: W. W. Norton, 1977) or *Glare* (New York: W. W. Norton, 1997) by A. R. Ammons, both book-length works. Fractal effects also can be found in my book *Sensual Math* (New York: W. W. Norton, 1995): see "Fuzzy Feelings," "Southbound in a Northbound Lane," and the sequence "Give."

3. Benoit Mandelbrot, *Fractals: Form, Chance, and Dimension* (San Francisco: W. H. Freeman, 1977), 4.

4. Alice Fulton, "Of Formal, Free, and Fractal Verse: Singing the Body Eclectic," *Poetry East* 21–22 (fall 1986), 200–213. Reprinted in *Feeling as a Foreign Language: The Good Strangeness of Poetry* (St. Paul, Minn.: Graywolf Press, 1999).

5. Ezra Pound, "A Few Don'ts by an Imagiste," *Poetry* 1 (1913) 200–206.

6. T. S. Eliot, "The Waste Land," *The Complete Poems and Plays 1909–1950* (New York: Harcourt, Brace & World, 1971), 37–55.

7. John H. Holland, *Hidden Order: How Adaptation Builds Complexity* (Reading, Mass.: Addison-Wesley, 1995).

8. M. Mitchell Waldrop, *Complexity: The Emerging Science at the Edge of Order and Chaos* (New York: Simon and Schuster, 1992), 12.

9. Waldrop, quoting John H. Holland in "Master of the Game," *Complexity* 147.

10. Eliot, "The Waste Land," 46.

11. Ezra Pound, "Canto LIV," *The Cantos of Ezra Pound* (London: Faber & Faber, 1954), 293.

12. John C. Thirlwall, quoting William Carlos Williams in "Ten Years of a New Rhythm," in William Carlos Williams, *Pictures from Brueghel and Other Poems* (New York: New Directions, 1962), 183.

13. Ezra Pound to Harriet Monroe, January 1915, *Letters, 1907–1941* (London: Faber & Faber, 1951), 183.

14. Pound, "A Few Don'ts," 204.

15. Marjorie Perloff, *Radical Artifice: Writing Poetry in the Age of Media* (Chicago: University of Chicago Press, 1991), 27–28.

16. Holland, *Hidden Order*, 11.

17. Eliot, "The Waste Land," 39.

18. Adrienne Rich, "Snapshots of a Daughter-in-Law," *Snapshots of a Daughter-in-Law: Poems 1954–1962* (New York: W. W. Norton, 1967), 22.

19. Alice Fulton, "Give: A Sequence Reimagining Daphne and Apollo," *Sensual Math* (New York: W. W. Norton, 1995), 71–113.

20. Pound, "A Few Don'ts," 203.

21. Ezra Pound, "A Retrospect," *Literary Essays* (New York: New Directions, 1954), 9.

22. Ezra Pound to T. S. Eliot, 24 December 1921, *Letters*, 234.

23. John Canaday, *What Is Art? An Introduction to Painting, Sculpture, and Architecture* (New York: Knopf, 1980), 205.

24. Reading, "Dynamical Symmetries."

25. Pound, "A Few Don'ts," 201.

26. James Gleick, *Chaos: Making a New Science* (New York: Viking Penguin, 1987), 106.

DANIEL TOBIN

A. R. Ammons and the Poetics of Chaos

A great disorder is an order.—Wallace Stevens, "Connoisseur of Chaos"

"A butterfly stirring in the air today in Peking can transform storm systems next month in New York."[1] James Gleick's pithy description of what has come to be known in chaos studies as the "butterfly effect," the notion that the most insignificant phenomenon can effect drastic changes in even the most apparently ordered system, exemplifies the kind of natural occasion that would attract the eccentric gaze of A. R. Ammons, whose work reveals at every turn its profound sympathy with the new science. Ammons finds his most precise and stirringly imaginative insights through his meditation on "dynamical systems." In such systems the poet not only discerns the seemingly random, "nonlinear" deviations from the expected pattern of order, but uncovers new orders arising spontaneously. Ammons's poetry thus embodies in its substance and style what Gleick might call a vision of "chaos and order together,"[2] and so his work is deeply mimetic of chaos's fundamental vision. It is at once imaginatively eccentric and, often, stylistically "nonlinear," as in such poems as "Corsons Inlet," where Ammons himself declares, "I have drawn no lines" in his quest for "narrow orders" (*Collected Poems* 149).

Therefore, as in physicist Stephen Smale's "topographies,"[3] Ammons's poems may be understood as "systems" that are at once "robust" and "strange"—robust because they hold together chaos and stability, order and disorder, and strange because they incorporate the unexpected, the unpredictable. Throughout Ammons's career his poetry manifests these essential properties, enabling his work to absorb its remarkable variety of perceptions as well as its stunning array of styles and diction. These properties, as in "global systems," give imaginative shape as well to his longer pieces *Sphere* and *Garbage*. Yet, as I hope to show by the end of this essay, Ammons's work not only represents an ingenious convergence of scientific perception and artistic composition, it signals a reinvention of Romantic sources of imagination. "Nature, the prime genial artist, inexhaustible in diverse powers, is equally inexhaustible in forms," Coleridge declared.[4] His insight is given a new and unexpected meaning in Ammons's "fields of order in disorder" (*Collected Poems* 151) where, as in the work of Wallace Stevens, we once again find ourselves more truly, and we find ourselves more strange.

The natural world as portrayed in Ammons's early lyrics anticipates many of the key concepts of chaos theory, and as such the more encompassing visions of *Sphere* and *Garbage*. Without question, the expressly scientific fascination with nature in Ammons's poetry has been evident from the publication in 1955 of his first book, *Ommateum*, which takes its name from the zoological term for an insect's compound eye.[5] Beyond Ammons's adoption of such highly technical scientific knowledge and terminology, his incorporation of science as a mode of perception gestures at a still more fundamental concern with nature's creative potential, as well as his own. In Ammons's vision, particular physical realities always come to intimate cosmic, even metaphysical concerns. In "Poetics," he writes: "I look for the way / things will turn out / spiralling from a center, / the shape / things will take to come forth in" (*Collected Poems* 199); and in "Saliences": "here / is this dune fest / releasing / mind feeding out, / gathering clusters, / fields of order in disorder, / where choice / can make beginnings" (*Collected Poems* 152). As both of these defining early poems suggest, the scanning eye of Ammons's own far-ranging imagination reveals a reality always in process, in which the poet's powers of creation depend on the recognition of their place within the ever-widening scope of the world's unquenchable generation. Both the world and the poet's rendering of it comprise what chaos theorists call a "dynamical system," a system in which apparently sharply defined patterns of order break down to form new unpredictable patterns that, instead of being purely random, actually form new, more complex patterns of organization—new provisional "shapes," or "clusters," or "centers" that come forth in what Stevens once called "an always incipient cosmos."

Given his propensity for discerning "order in disorder," perhaps it is no coincidence that Ammons's career takes shape during the same period in which such diverse theorists as Edward Lorenz, Mitchell Feigenbaum, Benoit Mandelbrot, and many others were evolving their ideas about the nature of chaos.[6] Moreover, as Katherine Hayles observes in her fine book *Chaos Bound*, within chaos theory not only is chaos seen "as order's precursor and partner," hidden order is understood to exist "within chaos itself."[7] Yet these attributes of what has come to be called (in part misleadingly) chaos theory, actually define two orientations of study: the "order-behind-chaos" school and the "order-out-of-chaos" school, the latter of which now more often goes by the name of "complexity theory."[8] As the name implies, the theorists of the "order-behind-chaos" school seek to explore the underlying order that may be inferred from apparently chaotic systems. Those associated with the "order-out-of-chaos" school explore complex systems that tend to hover between order and disorder, hoping to discern new orders emerging from seeming disorder. Significantly, we find both approaches present in the work of Ammons, in whose poems the synchronous insights of poet and scientist strike a remarkably insouciant harmony.

Perhaps this peculiarly fruitful coincidence of poetry and cutting-edge physics in Ammons's work ought to be understood not so much as an eccentric anomaly in contemporary literature but rather as one of the defining examples of literature's embrace of "the field concept." Again, as Katherine Hayles affirms, the field concept—the notion that reality "consists not in discrete objects located in space but rather of an underlying field whose interactions produce both objects and space"[9]—has had a profound influence on twentieth-century literature, through the work of writers as diverse as Henry Adams, Jorge Luis Borges, Doris Lessing, and Thomas Pynchon. For literary theorists like Hayles and writers such as John Barth,[10] the field concept is perhaps the central paradigm of our time, influencing literature and literary theory alike, shaping both the modern and postmodern literary milieus even while it cuts across various academic disciplines and cultural manifestations.[11] It is, as Foucault would define it, an epistime, a system of knowledge that seems to be everywhere present, from popular car commercials to the more innovative trends in contemporary poetry—witness Jorie Graham's *The Dream of the Unified Field*, winner of the 1996 Pulitzer Prize. As Hayles describes, essential to the field concept is the notion that things are interconnected in a kind of "cosmic web" of energy patterns. Reality is a "dance," an all-encompassing motion that ultimately dismisses the notion of a purely objective observer. It is only a short step between conceiving reality as a field and conceiving that field as a system of infinite complexity.

"How can we know the dancer from the dance," Yeats asked, and, as Ammons exults, "I will show you / the underlying that takes no image to itself, / cannot be shown or said, / but weaves in and out of moons and bladderweeds, / and is all and / beyond destruction because created fully in no / particular form."[12] This latter conception of nature as "all in all," as harbinger of "something more deeply interfused," is consistent with Ammons's roots in Romanticism, as is his emphasis on "the widening scope" of his own imaginative vision, which, as Steven Schneider astutely remarks, also places him in the tradition of Emerson, Whitman, and Thoreau.[13] Ammons's indisputable preoccupation with the discourses of science, combined with his interest in Romanticism, makes his poetry a remarkable contemporary crystallization that at once unites the disparate discourses of science and literature and likewise addresses itself to what is surely the original problem of Western thought: the relationship between order and chaos. Implicated deeply in the Western tradition, though perceived of as a formlessness that requires ordering, chaos nevertheless exerts a powerful allure as an idea bound to order's own origin, an idea without which creation itself would be meaningless.

This allure of chaos as something more than merely the antithesis of order and form is a central theme in Ammons's poems. It is, in fact, the primary condition of both natural and imaginative creation. "We are led on," he affirms in "This Misfit," "to the boundaries / where relations loosen into chaos" (*Collected Poems* 123). The poet, like Thomas Kuhn's scientist whose discoveries result in revolutionary new paradigms,[14] is the misfit whose fascination with peripheries, with the "raw blocks of material," reflects a still profounder conviction that the nature of creation itself is perhaps best discerned in the unformed. It is a notion intimated by the title itself, since to "misfit" the form of the poem, to rescue the product of imagination from too strict a closure, is to recognize its place in "an enlarging unity" that eludes total representation. As such, disorder is "ripe," as Ammons observes in "Identity," and "prodigal," for it discloses "orders moving in and out of orders, collisions / of orders, dispersions" (*Collected Poems* 77). It is in the dispersed, in the apparently formless, the chaotic, that perhaps a more compelling conception of order reveals itself. This conviction is given mythologized form in *Sphere*, where Ammons pictures chaos as a progenitor of order:

> Chaos stirred in himself,
> Spirals (cellular whirlwinds), upward swoops of bending aspiration,
> collisions high with potentials of linkage, dissolvings and
> meldings lengthy and free—these "motions" brought particles
> into progression often: if the progressions often failed into
> tatterdemalion, do-funnies, whatchamacallits, and thingumbobs,

there was time enough in the slow motions of landforms, oceans,
of moon and sun for Chaos to undo and recommence: certain
weaves caught on to random hooks and came into separations and

identity.
 (*Sphere* 33)

These lines from *Sphere* offer a typically tongue-in-cheek vision of the
role of disorder in the creation of order. It is a vision that foreshad-
ows Ammons's celebration of waste in *Garbage* as yet another avatar
of order in the wake of degeneration. Like the garden web of the early
poem "Identity," poetry paradoxically "keeps order at the center where
space is freest" (*Collected Poems* 115–16). From the outset of his work,
the order of poetry is conceived of by Ammons as being bound inextricably to the kind of radical freedom and elusive progression that
might best be understood as "nonlinear."

In nature, the radical freedom of nonlinear systems reflects a propensity for small causes to compound into effects well out of proportion to the original scale. In technical terms, they exhibit acute sensi-
tivity to initial conditions.[15] An example may be drawn from a recent
television commercial where, safe in their new Range Rover, newly-
weds pore frantically over their rumpled map on a deserted mountain road. "Nothing to worry about," the husband assures his wife.
Altogether elsewhere, in a swamp miles away, a hawk grips a turtle in
its claws and carries it off. High over the receding landscape it slips
free, bouncing shell-first onto a huge boulder at the top of a mountain, then landing on its feet below. The turtle, unharmed, hunkers
off. But the slightest tap of the turtle's shell has jarred loose the boulder from its precarious ridge. "We're not lost," the husband, still fum-
bling with the map, again assures his wife as the ground begins to
tremble underneath them, louder and louder, the boulder now roll-
ing directly at them down the road, now cresting in the windshield.
Madison Avenue notwithstanding, for the order-behind-chaos school
even such radical instances of disorder, if examined with the appropriate instrument, often reveal "little spikes of order." Still more startlingly, fine structures and indeed remarkably complex patterns, like
the infinite variety of snowflakes born "of imbalance in the flow of

energy from one piece of nature to another,"[16] often reveal themselves. As Alan Holder points out, in a similar way "order and disorder in Ammons do not typically occur in . . . purity or isolation," but "tend to be found together."[17] More emphatically than Holder suggests, however, the co-presence of order and disorder in Ammons's poetry suggests that the weather of his imagination naturally acclimates itself to such apparently chaotic richness, the very diversity of which occasions the poet's participation in the visionary field:

> I will show you
> the underlying that takes no image to itself,
> cannot be shown or said,
> but weaves in and out of moons or bladderweeds,
> is all and
> beyond destruction
> because created fully in no
> particular form
> (*Collected Poems* 115)

Certainly of all Ammons's early work, "Corsons Inlet" articulates most acutely his preoccupation with nature's "disorderly orders," as well as with what is so deeply yet elusively interfused in the whole widening scope of the field: the Overall. Walking among dunes along an inlet shore, the poet finds liberation in a "release from forms / from the perpendiculars, / straight lines, blocks, boxes, binds / of thought" (*Collected Poems* 148). The zigzag motion of the poem's lines down the page are intended to mirror both the motions of the poet's mind as it moves through its "eddies of meaning" and the elusive scope of the seashore itself in all the shifting amplitude of its flux. Here, the poet is not so much released from forms as from fixed forms of thought and being. Instead, through "the overall wandering of mirroring mind" in which he traces the clarified ephemera of the shore, all the while "erecting no boundaries," he discerns "an order held / in constant change" (*Collected Poems* 150). Unwilling, however, to indulge in the kind of speculation that would affirm an abstraction at the expense of living particulars, he declares, "Overall is beyond me" (*Collected Poems* 148). Clearly Ammons's "Overall" is not the same as

Emerson's "Oversoul," an abstraction that prizes transcendence over an immanence teeming with generation and decay.[18] What does get affirmed through the whole motion of the poem, however, is the process itself, what Alfred North Whitehead would have called the living "nexus of actual occasions" that compose reality.[19] The ultimate reality of "Corsons Inlet" is, as the poem itself suggests, "a congregation / rich with entropy: nevertheless, separable, noticeable / as one event, / not chaos . . . a 'field' of action / with moving, incalculable center" (*Collected Poems* 150). Quoting these lines, Roger Gilbert goes on to make explicit Ammons's affinity to chaos theory: "Complexity is not chaos."[20] In short, the "ultimate reality" for Ammons is not an order defined from above and entirely knowable, but something at most "noticeable" amidst the shifting flow or reality—a field unified paradoxically by grace of its very diversity.

From the widest scope of the macrocosm to the most intimate glimpse of the microcosm, "Corsons Inlet" revels in a system at once seemingly infinite in diversity and continuous in its integrity. Nevertheless, for Ammons, there is no "finality of vision," for the creative process, like the ecological process of his dune-swept shore, depends likewise on "the wider forces," the "enlarging grasps of disorder," out of which order itself is momentarily fastened. In short, in a manner consistent with Coleridge's insight on the nature of imagination, though far more radical in his organicism, Ammons would recapture in his poetry the living dynamic of nature. He would reveal through the *naturata* of its forms the *naturans* of the whole system, an aspiration whose very impossibility bears witness to the inexhaustible flow of reality itself.

Not surprisingly, then, in the early poem "Choice" Ammons invokes "the god / that rolls up circles of our linear / sight" (*Collected Poems* 35). On the one hand, Ammons implicitly refers here to our genetically programmed ability to see only within a very circumscribed band of lightwaves. On the other hand, his claim metaphorically implies a moral inadequacy—our tendency as humans to limit the scope of imagination, to circumscribe it within a limited valency. Linear sight would conceive a world of strict proportionality in which causes and their effects are congruent. In the scientific realm this is precisely the kind of Newtonian world that chaos theory has shown to be so limiting in its representation of reality. Chaos theory, as I have already remarked, demonstrates that such linearity is the exception, and that nonlinearity—a world of startlingly disproportionate relations between causes and effects—is in fact the norm.[21] That is why, as James Gleick points out, so many chaos theorists are fascinated by flow, which he defines as "shape plus change, motion plus form." What "dynamical shapes like flames and organic shapes like leaves" reveal, according to Gleick, is "some not yet understood weaving of forces" and, perhaps ultimately, "a connection between motion and universal form."[22] Flow is the dynamic conjoining set of form and motion.

The problem Ammons sets for himself in the long poems *Sphere* (tellingly subtitled "the form of a motion") and *Garbage* is to sustain just such dynamic flow or, as he himself declares, "a rugged variety of the formless formed" (*Sphere* 16). Characteristically, what fascinates him in both these capacious works are "the shapes nearest shapelessness," for it is such shapes that he says "awe us most" and "suggest the god" (*Sphere* 16). The god of *Sphere* is, of course, the same "nonlinear" god of "Choice" who inspires the poet, now in both these longer poems, to subvert the tight proportions of apparent form by allowing the fixed sections of each poem to flow into those that follow. Similarly, the three-line stanzas of *Sphere*, like the unrhymed couplets of *Garbage*, merely allude to traditional fixed forms. One might say that in the flow of both poems, linearity breaks free into nonlinearity to form more elaborate patterns of sense and organization. This is most evident in *Sphere* and *Garbage*, where the ongoing motion of the poet's meditations breaks free of each poem's delineated sections. It is as if the sections themselves were there to announce their provisional nature rather than to indicate to the reader any real sense of closure. They are like rocks in a stream whose currents flow back on themselves and each other even as the stream itself flows forward. Apparent order and apparent disorder mingle to form, in each poem, a seemingly self-generating flow that composes the poet's diverse observations of nature; shards of memory and history; news items; his own proprioceptive musings; swimmingly elaborated refluxes of philosophy, theology, science; as well as a range of diction from street slang to high Romantic rhetoric; into "narratives of motion" that he would simultaneously shape into the sustained whole of the poem. "These are the motions," Ammons affirms in *Garbage*, "this is the dance," suggesting that the art of the poem itself derives from the poet's organization of his material into intensely complex patterns across assumed boundaries.

In *Sphere*, Ammons's penchant for creating complex patterns becomes evident at the poem's outset. *Sphere* begins with a meditation on the "sexual basis of all things rare," which in succeeding sections quickly modulates to contemplations on thought itself, or the relationship between "knowledge and carnal knowledge," and finally on death as dramatized by "the vultures' pull and gulp," as well as the work of "the lessening transformers" (*Sphere* 11). These opening sections establish what is the poem's central recurrent theme: the necessary coexistence of creation and destruction and its meaning for human consciousness. The mutual processes of birth and death—the godlike forces now divorced from myth, though periodically mythologized throughout the poem—are the omnipresent muses of physical reality. Not surprisingly, near the poem's end, Ammons reiterates his initial meditation by claiming that male and female are the two principles that give birth to the mind and presumably to the poem. Throughout the poem's 155 twelve-line sections, Ammons plays riffs on this encompassing theme through a series of meditations, speculations, and vignettes that range from musings on the misguided ideas of New York City writers, to the launch of Apollo 16, to the Most High, to a catbird perched on the jungle gym nearby his vegetable garden. For Ammons, these discrete occasions, seemingly unconnected, are bound to each other as pervasively as is the physical universe to itself, the universe that holds in dynamic relation the totality of single things. Again, the key word here is "dynamic," for what Ammons abhors above all else is a static unity. As always it is the relationship between the one and the many, the center and the periphery, that forms the primary axis of Ammons's poetic, with its seemingly infinite vectors of knowledge and experience. From this perspective, *Sphere* is the embodiment of the poem as complex system.

Indeed, it is the wondrous complexity of material reality that Ammons would seek to mirror in the poem, a complexity so stirring to his imagination that *Sphere* would create a bridge between the scientific world and the world of religion. From one perspective, "the scope of oneness under which / the proud ephemerals play discretely their energizing / laws and play out" (*Sphere* 38) bears witness to the splendor of the universe's physical cosmogenesis, as well as its ongoing transformations within the infinitely complex and variable field of space-time. From another perspective—though really *through* this primary perspective—matter itself is "a mere seed afloat in radiance" (*Sphere* 39). Ammons's claim here echoes the vision of scientist and mystic Teilhard de Chardin, who saw the universe as a "divine milieu" in which matter and spirit exist in a mysterious and transfiguring communion. Ammons is not so very far from that vision when he writes, "in the comprehensiveness and focus of the Most High is the obliteration / total that contains all and in that we rest" (*Sphere* 39). Both the scientist-mystic and the scientist-poet apprehend in material existence the lineaments of the spirit. Ammons, of course, has no interest in aligning his vision with Christian doctrine, and in particular the spiritualization of matter implied by the doctrine of the incarnation. The materials *are* materials for Ammons, and not grounds for religious confirmation. The cosmic forces are cosmic forces, and science is the symbolic system in which Ammons has his primary imaginative life.

Nevertheless, in *Sphere* (and elsewhere) he shows himself to be profoundly conversant with the symbols of faith. What is born of this remarkable union of science and religion is a kind of hybrid consciousness in which the supernatural eternity of religion is displaced by what Ammons repeatedly calls "the ongoing" and "the ongoing mind," which is at once immanent in material reality and yet transcends our full comprehension: "the highest god / we never meet, essence out of essence, motion without motion" (*Sphere* 17). Not unlike the contemplative's steady prayer, the poem's job is to instill in the reader a kind of equipoise or focus, the singular repetition of the highest god's fusion of stillness and movement:

> The purpose of the motion of a poem is to bring the focused,
> Awakened mind to no-motion, to a still contemplation of the
> Whole motion, all the motions, of the poem. . . .
> (*Sphere* 40)

I use the word "repetition" above as a purposeful echo of Coleridge's definition of the imagination: "a repetition in the finite mind of the eternal act of creation in the infinite I Am."[23] What we find in Ammons's declaration of a poem's purpose is the same kind of understanding of the relationship between macrocosm and microcosm that predicates Coleridge's conception of the imagination. Likewise, both poets are concerned to align what Ammons calls in *Garbage* the poet's "action of making" with the wider reality of an "eternal" creation. The key difference is that whereas Coleridge's view of imagination finds its model in biblical sources, Ammons looks toward the revelations of modern physics, as well as his own intuited understanding of the nature of reality, for his conception of poetry's place in the cosmic scheme. As such, while it would be wrong to read into *Sphere* evidence of a new "natural supernaturalism," it nevertheless seems obvious that Ammons's enterprise in the poem is, in part, to synthesize this key aspect of the Romantic tradition and to adapt it both to our turbulent time and to his own poetic needs.

Ammons's cross-fertilization of modern physics with his own version of the romantic imagination is perhaps most clearly evident in *Sphere* when he claims, "There is a faculty or knack, smallish, in the mind that can turn / as with tooling irons immediacy into bends of concision, shapes / struck with airs to keep" (*Sphere* 42). Coleridge called the imagination an "esemplastic" or shaping power. Yet again there are differences. Ammons calls this faculty "smallish," a reconfiguration that tempers any pretense toward the "glorious faculty" of Wordsworth's revelation on Mount Snowdon at the end of *The Prelude*. Nevertheless, *Sphere* can ring with the old Wordsworthian grandeur: "the real force of the gods returns to its heights

/ where it dwells, its everlasting home" (*Sphere* 48). Similarly, when Ammons surveys the cheated, maimed, afflicted, the castaways of society, he declares "I know them: I love them: I am theirs," a proclamation that resounds with Whitman's uncanny powers of identification. To be sure, identity is another central theme of *Sphere*, as is the poet's ability to negotiate between the claims of identity and the claims of a reality that exists in constant flow both below and above the solid appearances of the world. The poet's exploration of this theme brings him to a recognition of the fundamental pathos of conscious life: "We want to change without changing." Every line of *Sphere* ultimately resonates with this paradox, for on the one hand Ammons sings the identification of the one and the many ("crush a bug and the universe goes hollow / with hereafter"), while on the other he prizes the radically individual nature of existence: "you have your identity when / you find out not what you can keep your mind on but what / you can't keep your mind off" (*Sphere* 57–58).

Likewise, then, *Sphere* at once "insists on differences," yet these "contours of staying" must finally commune in a harmony that "can be recognized in the highest / ambience of diversity" (*Sphere* 57–58). At its most insistent, what *Sphere* awakens us to is that each of us, and not just the poet, "stands in the peak and center / of perception," at once a discrete and yet an intimate part of the whole. Ultimately, for the Ammons of *Sphere*, we are called to "make a home of motion" in actions that would to our best abilities accomplish the ideal equipoise between identification and difference. As such, the Ferris wheel Ammons introduces at the end of the poem stands at once as an intact, discernible form and a figure that is not only in motion but *is* its motion. It is at once the orb of the earth and of its inhabitants. We are at once "ourselves," discrete individuals, and we are "sailing," a part of the ongoing; and so, in the best sense, the vision that ends *Sphere* is Ammons's mundane version of Dante's whirling heavenly kaleidoscope at the end of his *Divine Comedy*, a figure that unites the transcendent and immanent worlds. Achieved through Ammons's understanding of the deep structure of reality, and not through the supernatural, the wheel is the symbolic answer to the question he voices earlier in the poem: "How do you fare and how may we fare to Thee?"

If, as its title suggests, *Sphere* means to quicken the reader's reverence for the dynamic order that both underlies and at times seems to emerge from the flux of reality, it does so without negating the forces of limitation and, in particular, death. Indeed, the ongoing process of loss is integral to that vital, underlying order, an essential aspect of what Ammons calls "the mystery." The work of the poet's imagination must therefore engage the fact that there is no birth without death, that sooner or later everything becomes part of an immense waste. In *Sphere*, Ammons embraces this essential aspect of the nature of things when he writes, "I want to be the shambles, / the dump, the hills of good the bulldozer shoves, so gulls / in carrion-gatherings can fan my smouldering" (*Sphere* 68). Written nearly twenty years after *Sphere*, *Garbage* is the elaborate creation of Ammons's glancing wish. Where *Sphere* announces a vision of the whole and begins with a meditation on the sources of life in sexual union, *Garbage* announces a vision of decay and begins with a march of "creepy little creepers," harbingers of death, who in a brilliant transformation become the poet's insinuating muses. Decomposition is the true, unheralded source of composition that Ammons will now celebrate. "If you've derived from life, a going thing called life," Ammons concludes near the poem's end, "life has a right to derive life from you" (*Garbage* 98–99). From this ethical standpoint, the key conception of life as a complex web of mutuality so central to *Sphere* reappears in *Garbage*, only now Ammons's vantage is even more stridently from the ground up rather than from the pinnacle of the whole.

Consistent with Ammons's Heraclitean desire to make the way down the way up, *Garbage* moves through its eighteen sections by extending further his approach of organizing *Sphere* as a sequence of brilliantly rambling meditations and vignettes. Fat Minnie Fuhrer, a colleague dying of cancer, Ole Liza who used to work in the fields of Ammons's childhood, all become woven into the poem's flow that would, as in *Sphere*, assimilate itself into "the ongoing." One of the most moving of these vignettes is Ammons's vivid description of his own father, slumped and strapped in his wheelchair shortly before his death from diabetes. Here we find the inverse of the Ferris wheel, that final vision of motion and stillness upon which *Sphere* itself turns.

Mulling over the wheels with the other men dying in the ward, Ammons's father appears an image of stasis, of life's final heartbreaking waste. Again, the poet is driven to reconcile the particular with the inexorable motion of the whole. What we find in *Garbage*, then, is not merely an elaboration of themes already explored earlier in *Sphere* and his short lyrics, but a new and necessary confrontation with "the gap" between Ammons's vision of dynamic unity—the whole motion intimated in its discrete forms—and the integrity of those forms in themselves. The spirit, as Ammons observes, may be forever, "the residual and informing energy," but what about "this manifestation, this man, this incredible flavoring and / building up of character and eclat, gone . . . a local / event, infinitely unrepeatable?" (*Garbage* 38). Thus, while *Garbage* would bear witness to "the spindle of energy" that runs through all things from high to low, from "boulders to dead stars," the poem positively requires the messiness of its many tangents.

Of course, Ammons cannot fill in the gap the poem implicitly opens throughout his ruminations on everything from galaxies, to language, to the poem itself regarded reflexively as though in mid-composition; and so it is the gap between whole and part itself that, in effect, generates surpluses of meaning both in the poem and, as Ammons would have it, in reality. The infinitely complex system of the universe is in essence a garbage dump that recycles itself in an everlasting communion among its diverse parts. As such, the conflict between the "order-behind-chaos" school and the "order-out-of-chaos" school is simply a moot point for Ammons. From the poet's perspective, in "the crux of matter" both are true. Faced with our own dissolution, the poet calls us to "an ease beyond our understanding" because it is the very nature of the universe to call us out of our egocentrism into a plenitude that eludes any totalizing conception:

> forms are never
>
> permanent form, change the permanence, so
> that one thing one day is something else another
>
> day, and the energy that informs all forms just
> breezes right through filth as clean as a whistle:

all this stuff here is illusory, you know, and
while it gives you bad dreams and wilding desires

and sometimes makes you spit up at night, it is
the very efflorescence of the fountain of shapes. . . .
    (*Garbage* 115)

Ammons's "ease that passes understanding" is a reconsideration of
Eliot's promised peace, though in Ammons's version the wasteland
is anything but arid. Instead, the decomposition of individual forms
carries within itself the potential for positive rebirth. Samsara, our
world of illusion, as some Buddhists say, becomes Nirvana, the condition of enlightened being, in the moment of transformed vision that
supervenes our old paradigms of thought.

It is a similar belief in the mind's capacity to attain transforming
vision that shapes the wider aim of *Garbage*. For this reason, one of
Ammons's most prominent objects of concern in the poem is poetry
itself, as well as the poet's action of making. "Art," as Ammons reminds
us, "makes shape, order, meaning, / purpose where there was none,
or none discernible, / none derivable" (*Garbage* 67), and this mean-
ing-making function is the very stuff of life; and the stuff of life, as
Ammons continually takes pains to remind us, is garbage. When he
recounts the beginnings of a poem developing in the mind in section
six, the process culminates in "a brutal burning—a rich, raw urgency"
that mimics both the body's own production of "waste" and the laws
of necessity that form volcanoes. Ammons here is neither being ironic
nor indulging in hyperbole. Governed by the poem's overarching
conceit, everything is both waste and generation. Poetry itself is "like
an installation at Marine / shale: it reaches down into the dead pit /
and cool oil of recognition and words" into the "stringy gook" of what
lies below our conscious minds (*Garbage* 108). The purpose of that
descent is to remind the mind of its vital relationship to "communication channels" that lead well out beyond its own inner workings into
the wider universe of which it is a part. In the fullest sense, *Garbage*
is an epic of the mind's quest for what Wordsworth called the love that
"subsists all lasting grandeur," though in Ammons's version that grandeur includes the least likely elements of the sublime—trash and bird-

shit as well as "our cold / killing brothers the stars"—all of which must be held in our "right regard." To attain as much is to recall the ideal Ammons articulated twenty years earlier in *Sphere*. It is to embrace a hope for each of us poised at the peak and center of perception:

> have
> you stopped to think what existence is, to be here
>
> no where so much has been or is yet to come and
> where isness itself is just the name of a segment
>
> of flow: stop, think: millennia jiggle in your eyes
> at night, the twinklers, eye and star. . . .
>   (*Garbage* 48)

"Pattern born amid formlessness: that is biology's basic beauty and its basic mystery": so James Gleick summarizes the role of chaos in the formation of life.[24] The same words could adequately describe Ammons's radically organic aesthetic in *Sphere* and *Garbage*. In a profound sense, Ammons's use of such scientific insights likewise represents the fullest application of organicism's ideal of internally realized form. Here again is Coleridge on the difference between mechanic and organic form:

> The form is mechanic when on any given material we impress a pre-determined form, not necessarily arising out of the properties of the material, as when to a mass of red clay we give it whatever shape we wish it to retain when hardened. The organic form, on the other hand, is innate; it shapes as it develops itself from within, and the fulness of its development is one and the same with the perfection of its outward form. Such is the life, such is the form. Nature, the prime genial artist, inexhaustible in diverse powers, is equally inexhaustible in forms.[25]

Ammons might have had this famous passage in mind when in *Sphere* he explicitly eschews the poem conceived of as "the painted gourd on the mantelpiece" for the poem conceived of as a dynamic flow, the purpose of which as stated earlier "is to bring the focused, / awakened mind to no-motion, to a still contemplation of the / whole motion, all the motions, of the poem" (*Sphere* 40). To read the poem in this manner is to accept the poem as a "self-referential system" or "field" in which "the sense of moving along, coming closer to an end point, is revealed not exactly as an illusion but as a half-truth as the seeker merges with the sought, the periphery with the center, the journey with its end."[26] This complex interpenetration of self, world, and language in the dynamic field of the poem precludes atomization because to enter the poem at all is to enter an evolving motion, a field that would compose its own ever-widening hermeneutical circle of the seeker and the sought, of reader and poem. Typically for Ammons, the blueprint for this expansive relationship is found in nature, as this passage from *Sphere* suggests:

> though the surface is crisp with pattern still we know
> that there are generalized underlyings, planes of substratum
> lessening from differentiation: under all life, fly and
>
> dandelion, protozoan, bushmaster, and ladybird, tendon
> and tendril (excluding protocellular organelles) is the same
> cell: and under the cell is water, a widely generalized
>
> condition, and under that energy and under that perhaps
> the spirit of the place . . .
>
>   our selves float here.
> (*Sphere* 14–15)

What *Sphere* affirms above all are "the mirrorments" that bind together discrete existence with the whole field of becoming that at once underlies and overlies our human condition: each of us stands at the peak and center of perception. Human beings exist in the liminal space where microcosm and macrocosm meet. In a radical way, *Sphere* and *Garbage* deny the absolute distinction between the poem as a mirror of nature and the poem as lamp, the pure product of the poet's imagination. The mirror is the lamp, the lamp is the mirror, for what both poems finally embody in their whole motion is "the recursive power of flows within flows," the multifarious unity of "similarities across scales," of "patterns inside patterns."[27] To be sure, Ammons appears to echo such ideas directly in the poem when he writes "though the surface is crisp with pattern still we know / that there are generalized underlyings, planes of substratum / lessening from differentiation" (*Sphere* 14). Here, again, Ammons sounds remarkably like an "order-behind-chaos" theorist, proclaiming "the one cell" underlying all things. Yet, when later in the poem he observes, "keep jiggling the innumerable elements and / even integrations can fall out of disintegrations," he appears to echo the "order-out-of-chaos" school. Again, for Ammons, there is no contradiction since in his reality, though chaos is "the ampler twin" of order, always "the visible, coherent, discrete dwell / in flotation which faces out on the illimitable" (*Sphere* 71).

Similarly, Ammons's preoccupation with relationships of scale in both nature and poetry is evident in the grand shifts of perception, from microscopic and subatomic to galactic and universal, that characterize both poems as well as the whole of his work. Indeed, his range of poetic production, from the shortest lyrics to his book-length works, embodies this concern as a matter of form as well as theme. What we find in Ammons's poetry, then, and particularly in *Sphere* and *Garbage*, is his embrace of complex forms; to be sure, the kind of complex forms that are characteristic of chaotic systems as found in nature.[28] The measurement of regular forms such as circles and rectangles remains unaffected by the scale of the instrument used to measure them. If the diameter of a particular circle is one inch, it will be so whether you measure it with a yardstick or a ruler. As Katherine Hayles points out, this is not the case with irregular forms like coastlines or the human vascular system.[29] In such complex forms, measurements increase as the scales decrease so that, as Benoit Mandelbrot, the founder of fractal geometry, realized, in such forms infinite space exists within a finite space.[30] As such, the more you measure a coastline, like Corsons Inlet, for example, by "breaking" it into discrete segments, the more it reveals self-similar details that project into infinity. The idea recalls Zeno's paradox, where an arrow fired at its target theoretically never reaches its mark since the path of its flight may be divided an infinite number of times. In a sense, fractal geometry confirms the "widening scope" Ammons affirms not only in "Corsons Inlet" but in *Sphere* and *Garbage* as well. Though "Overall" is ultimately beyond him—"the mind cannot visualize the whole self-embedding of complexity"[31]—he nevertheless glimpses a partial infinity implied by recursive symmetries between scales. In fact, his poems are predicated upon such symmetries.

On a still grander scale, *Garbage* organizes its patterns of recurrent images and themes according to a similar embrace of complex form. The mound of garbage that looms like a ziggurat at the opening of the poem, churning new orders on a microscopic scale out of our human waste, finds a self-similar mount of "celestial garbage" at the poem's end, both of which reiterate the further self-reflexive fact that "there is a mound, / too, in the poet's mind dead language is hauled / off to and burned down on, / the energy held and / shaped into new turns and clusters, / the mind / strengthened by what it strengthens" (*Garbage* 20). In these lines, what might be called the "fractal organization" of the poem—its tendency to arrive at its shape organically through the poet's hypersensitive attraction to the partial, the particular, and the marginal, as well as his willingness to delay the reader as a way of inferring the whole—becomes specifically implicated in the poet's creation of new orders out of an apparent chaos. In any case, the complexity of the interconnections among the poem's strands of theme or imagery hearken back to the still more perfect symmetry discovered in nature:

> we are natural: nature, not
>
> we, gave rise to us: we are not, though, though
> natural, divorced from higher, finer configurations:
>
> tissues and holograms of energy circulate in
> us and seek and find representations of themselves
>
> outside us, so that we can participate in
> celebrations high and know reaches of feeling
>
> and sight and thought that penetrate (really
> penetrate) far, far beyond these our wet cells,
>
> right on up past our stories, the planets, moons,
> and other bodies locally to the other end of

the pole where matter's forms diffuse and
energy loses all means to express itself except

as spirit. . . .
    (*Garbage* 21)

As Steven Schneider observes, these lines reveal Ammons's over-whelming desire to place even personal grief and suffering—what Teilhard de Chardin called in another context "the passivities of our diminishments"—within the context of a wider cosmic vision.[32] Or, as Ammons observed in *Sphere*, "we are not half-in and / half-out of the universe but unmendably integral" (*Sphere* 43).

Ammons's vision of a universe that forms an integral whole, not in spite of, but precisely through its infinite diversity, has remained consistent throughout his career. A conception of unity without di-versity, as he takes pains to remind us in the early poem "One:Many," is debilitating to the imagination. The "abstract one," the false "unity unavailable to change," leads to destruction. "Not unity by the win-nowing out of difference, / not unity thin and substanceless as abstrac-tion" (*Garbage* 38), he reiterates. Similarly, in *Sphere*, Ammons's con-cern with "the one:many problem" as he calls it, leads him to declare that "if there are / no boundaries that hold firm, everything can be ground into / everything else" (*Sphere* 61). Here, Ammons sounds as if he might be drawing the kind of conclusion consistent with some-one who has thought long and hard about the kind of chaotic turbu-lence that emerges from the slight alteration of the most determined system—"for want of a nail the shoe was lost" and so, by increments, is the entire battle. At the same time he can ask the question, "when does water seeping into the roothairs / pass the boundary after which it is a tree?" (*Sphere* 21). On the one hand, from slight alterations or-der may devolve into chaos; on the other, from the "chaos" of minute particulars an encompassing order emerges. What Ammons seeks to maintain in such apparently contradictory statements is not simply a balance between unity and diversity but the embodiment of a para-dox: how can one be many, how can many be one? Rather than run to any "easy victory," as he says in "Corsons Inlet," he would keep his readers alive in the paradox—the very same paradox that, like Blake in the palm of a hand, or Mandelbrot in a coastline, can hold infinity in a finite space. As James Gleick writes of the chaos theorists, "They had an eye for pattern, especially for pattern that appeared on different scales at the same time.... They are looking for the whole."[33] The same ought to be said of Ammons, whose sense of the whole is inextricable from his sense of the many.

Moreover, as I suggested earlier, the relationship of one to many is of moral significance to Ammons. As he wryly observes in *Sphere*, "they ask why I'm so big on the / one:many problem, they never saw one: my readers what do they / expect from a man born and raised in a country whose motto is *E / pluribus unum*?" (*Sphere* 65). The problem attracts not only Ammons's thoughts on the nature of reality and poetry, it reflects intimately the nature of our society. In *Garbage*, Ammons pushes his preoccupation with the relationship between one and many still further:

> if there is to be any regard for
>
> human life, it will have to be ours, right regard
> for human life including all other forms of life,
>
> including plant life: when we eat the body of
> another animal, we must undergo the sacrifice
>
> of noticing that life has been spent into our
> life, and we must care, then, for the life we
>
> have and for the life our life has cost, and we
> must make proper acknowledgements and sway some
>
> with reverence for the cruel and splendid tissue
> biospheric....
>   (*Garbage* 117–18)

These lines do more than restate the ecological vision articulated by Ammons in "Extremes and Moderations"; they recast the one:many problem within a still wider moral framework, a framework that similarly encompasses the celebration of human diversity. Once again, what we find in *Sphere* and *Garbage*, as throughout Ammons's work, is a poetry of elaborated and constantly reconfiguring patterns across multiple scales of experience. In a sense, these poems are constructed like huge attractors that perform the tensive union of the one and the many in a manner that would imitate, as far as language is able, the deep structure of physical reality.

An attractor, as Katherine Hayles explains, "is any point within an orbit that seems to attract the system to it."[34] In nature, the dynamics of such systems as a swinging pendulum or one's heartbeat are determined by such points. In the case of the pendulum, all motion tends to rest at the midpoint; in the case of one's heartbeat, any limited disturbance (with the exception of a massive heart attack) returns to its characteristic rhythm. In the case of what chaos theorists call a "strange attractor"—an attractor whose pattern of organization appears to lack any discernible idea of order—the apparently random cycles of systems as varied as fluid turbulence, viral outbreaks, schizophrenic eye movements, stock-market prices, and a dripping faucet in fact reveal a deep structure in which disorder "is mixed with clear remnants of order."[35] It is as if, paradoxically, randomness generated order, as if the peripheral through its very marginality gave rise to a shifting though nevertheless definable center. Chaos thus may be conceived as a dynamic motion that binds together the pure freedom of the apparently random and the organizational necessity of the seemingly intended. In *Sphere* and *Garbage*, it is as if the deep structure of both poems were modeled on such a conception of order emerging out of disorder, widely swinging arcs of thought, discursive patternings of ideas and images, vignettes, excursions that nonetheless cohere—"minor forms," as Ammons himself states, "within larger constructs" (*Garbage* 66). Here again, Ammons betrays an inclination toward a vision of order-out-of-chaos. Perhaps not surprisingly, then, the figure of "the center" recurs in both poems, not as a conceit that would rush the poem to an abstract closure, but as a kind of "strange attractor" that allows the poem to range over wide expanses of experience, while retaining its coherent, albeit complex organic form. "Touch the universe anywhere you touch it / everywhere," Ammons declares (*Sphere* 72). In other words, as if to answer the common postmodern claim that the desire for "the center" is merely nostalgic, the poem bears witness to the idea that any part may become "a living center" that would connect you to the ongoing motion of the whole.

Yet even while Ammons appears attracted to creating such complex unities in *Sphere* and *Garbage*, he nevertheless continually confronts processes that would seem to disturb the symmetry of the whole. These are the fearful symmetries of entropy and death. "How can and how long can an identity / hold to the skin of the earth?" Ammons asks in *Sphere* (*Sphere* 23). In one of that poem's most moving passages, the poet's reflection on the universe's "long, empty freezing gulfs" caught in the grip of entropy segues into the time "when the younger brother sickened and then moved no more." This interfusion of the most impersonal of deaths with the death of the poet's own brother would make death itself perhaps the strangest of strange attractors, drawing the cosmic and the particular alike into the orbit of its dark center. Without diminishing such "terrible transformations," Ammons would make death itself an occasion for exploring the positive implications of our natures as perishable beings. "In your end is my beginning," Ammons repeats over again in *Garbage*. The play on Eliot's refrain in *Four Quartets*—"in my beginning is my end, in my end is my beginning"—clearly intends to dislodge the self's quest for wholeness and even holiness from its reliance on self alone, the egocentric "my" giving way to an acknowledgement of the other, the "you" without whom there is no connection. Instead, Ammons would underscore that "we are bound together by our ends," and knowing as much, "we begin to / see the end of disturbing endlessness" (*Garbage* 63). Ultimately, the fact of death, both cosmic and personal, clarifies Ammons's implied network of mutuality. To this extent we are "trash," perishable, subject to dissolution and decay, though nonetheless "plenty wondrous." Toward the end of *Garbage*, Ammons pushes this insight even further:

> it's a wonder natural
> selection hasn't thinned out anything not perfectly
>
> beautiful: but nature, if I may speak for it,
> likes a broad spectrum approaching disorder so

as to maintain the potential of change with
variety and environment: the true shape of

perfect beauty, hard to find, somehow floats
implicit and stable there. . . .
    (*Garbage* 101)

Just as in the final pages of *The Origin of Species* Darwin celebrates
the grandeur of life that brings forth "endless forms most beautiful,"[36]
so here Ammons links an almost Platonic idea of the beautiful to the
diversity of life cast as it is against the relief of particular deaths. In
both cases, observations of physical processes obtained through science converge with revelations normally considered within the prov-
ince of the spiritual.

Indeed, Ammons directly addresses the metaphysical implications
of his poetic forays into physical reality when in *Sphere* he asks the
following question: "How to / devise a means that assimilates small
inspirations in a / large space, network, reticulation complex . . . but
moved forward by a controlling motion, design symmetry, / suasion,
so that harmony can be recognized in the highest / ambience of diversity?" (*Sphere* 58). The question Ammons poses in *Sphere* is essentially answered by the complex form of the poem itself, with its re-
quirement that the reader discern the poem's wider symmetry
precisely through its ambience of diversity. Still more significantly, it
could be the question asked by chaos theorists trying to catch a
glimpse of the universal across multiple scales of existence. Should
we push the implications further, it would be the question the universe asks itself in elaborating its own immense design, were it somehow conscious of its own ends and beginnings. And, if one were to
assume a theological perspective, it is the question that predicates the
origin of creation itself. Ultimately, Ammons's exploration of this
question from the latter standpoint is precisely what distinguishes
Garbage from *Sphere*. To be sure, *Sphere* conjures images of cosmogony in ways that pique the religious imagination, but not so
boldly as does *Garbage* where, from the outset, the waste mound that
serves as the work's recurring center and conceit is pictured as a sa-

cred pyramid up which garbage trucks circle as they "intone the morning," their garglings becoming unlikely prayers.

Such figurations hearken back to Ammons's first poems, with their appeal to the mythic sources of Sumer, a source revisited in the poems of *Sumerian Vistas*.[37] At the same time, Ammons's concern in *Garbage* with the relationship between energy and form, and of both to spirit, brings to full expression his work's remarkable convergence of the imaginative resources of science and religion:

> this is just a poem with a job to do: and that
>
> is to declare, however roundabout, sideways,
> or meanderingly (or in those ways) the perfect
>
> scientific and materialistic notion of the
> spindle of energy: when energy is gross,
>
> rocklike, it resembles the gross, and when
> fine it mists away into mystical refinements,
>
> sometimes passes right out of material
> recognizability and becomes, what?, motion,
>
> spirit, all forms translated into energy, as at
> the bottom of Dante's hell all motion is
>
> translated into form. . . .
>   (*Garbage* 24–25)

For Ammons, the reciprocity that exists between matter and spirit—spirit itself being, so it seems, a more rarified form of energy—so inheres in his sacred mound that he can portray his truck driver crying "holy, holy / holy" as he flicks his cigarette in a "spiritual swoop" to where "the consummations gather." Yet Ammons is not content merely to assert this intimate connection between matter and spirit. Rather, throughout the poem he further speculates on its nature:

>   oh, yes, yes, the matter goes on,
>
> turning into this and that, never the same thing
> twice: but what about the spirit, does it die

in an instant, being nothing in an instant out of
matter, or does it hold on to some measure of

time, not just the eternity in which it is not,
but does death go on being death of a billion
years—to infinity:
    (*Garbage* 37–38)

"This spirit was forever / and is forever, the residual and informing /
energy," he goes on to declare, as though once again to echo Teilhard
de Chardin: "In each of us, through matter, the whole history of the
world is in part reflected . . . by the totality of the energies of the
earth."[38]

Even so, despite so harmonious a vision, in *Garbage* Ammons
would once again step back from the easy victory of claiming to have
attained "Overall." The human world inevitably "trims the spirit too
sharply back," and even the poet's words, "which attach to edges, cannot / represent wholeness, so if all is all, the it / just is" (*Garbage* 114).
Finally, for Ammons, to capture the sacredness of everything in words
is an impossibility, just as for the chaos theorist, the conception of
universality across scales will always remain limited by the human
mind's finitude. Nevertheless, as the poet observes, though we may
"kick the *l* out of wor*l*d and cuddle / up with the avenues and byways
of the word," we are still "not alone in language" though "we may be
alone in words" (*Garbage* 50). Such an expanded notion of language
as an integral aspect of the motions of reality and not merely a prov-
ince of human creation at once chastens the presumption of those
who would, in Ammons's words, make it "fashionable to mean nothing" and at the same time enables us to affirm that "there is truly *only*
meaning, / only meaning, meanings, so many meanings, / meaning-
lessness becomes what to make of so many / meanings" (*Garbage* 86).
To assume as much enables us to widen the scope of our own vision,
to see the poet's words as helping us to fend for ourselves and each
other, and for the world—and finally, to paraphrase Wallace Stevens,
to see in our own chaotic time the ghostlier demarcations of a keener
idea of order.

1. James Gleick, *Chaos: The Making of a New Science* (New York: Viking, 1987), 8.
2. Ibid.
3. See Gleick, *Chaos*, 45–53.
4. S. T. Coleridge, *Selected Poetry and Prose* (New York: New American Library, 1951), 433.
5. Steven P. Schneider, *A. R. Ammons and the Poetics of Widening Scope* (Madison, N.J.: Fairleigh Dickinson University Press, 1994), 21.
6. See Gleick, *Chaos*, 35.
7. N. Katherine Hayles, *Chaos Bound: Orderly Disorder in Contemporary Literature and Science* (Ithaca: Cornell University Press, 1990), 9.
8. See Steven Johnson, "Strange Attraction," *Lingua Franca* (March/April 1996): 42–50; John Barth, "Chaos Theory: PostMod Science, Literary Model," in *Further Fridays: Essays, Lectures and Other Non-Fiction, 1984–1994* (Boston: Little, Brown, 1995), 328–42.
9. Hayles, *Chaos Bound*, xi.
10. See N. Katherine Hayles, *The Cosmic Web: Scientific Field Strategies and Literary Strategies in the Twentieth Century* (Ithaca: Cornell University Press, 1984); Barth, *Further Fridays*, 328–42.
11. See Hayles, *Chaos Bound*, 3–5; *Cosmic Web*, 9.
12. Ammons, *Selected Poems* (New York: Norton, 1986), 28.
13. See Schneider, *A. R. Ammons*, 15.
14. See Thomas Kuhn, *The Structure of Scientific Revolutions*, 2nd ed. (Chicago: University of Chicago Press, 1970).
15. See Hayles, *Chaos Bound*, 11.
16. Gleick, *Chaos*, 314.
17. Alan Holder, *A. R. Ammons* (New York: Twayne, 1978), 48.
18. See Schneider, *A. R. Ammons*, 84.
19. Alfred North Whitehead, *Adventures in Ideas* (New York: Macmillan, 1933), 258.
20. Roger Gilbert, "A. R. Ammons," in *Dictionary of Literary Biography: American Poets since World War II*, 4th series, ed. Joseph Conte (Detroit: Gale Research, 1996), 23.
21. Hayles, *Chaos Bound*, 11.
22. Gleick, *Chaos*, 195–96.
23. Coleridge, *Selected Poetry and Prose*, 263.
24. Gleick, *Chaos*, 299.

25. Coleridge, *Selected Poetry and Prose*, 432–33.

26. Hayles, *Cosmic Web*, 150–51.

27. Gleick, *Chaos*, 195, 103.

28. Hayles, *Chaos Bound*, 12–13.

29. Ibid., 12.

30. See Gleick, *Chaos*, 100.

31. Ibid.

32. Schneider, *A. R. Ammons*, 223–24.

33. Gleick, *Chaos*, 5.

34. Hayles, *Chaos Bound*, 147.

35. Gleick, *Chaos*, 147.

36. Charles Darwin, *The Origin of Species* (New York: New American Library, 1958), 460.

37. A. R. Ammons, *Sumerian Vistas* (New York: Norton, 1987).

38. Teilhard de Chardin, *Divine Milieu* (New York: Harper and Row, 1960), 59.

WORKS CITED

Ammons, A. R. *Collected Poems, 1951–1971*. New York: Norton, 1972.
———. *Garbage*. New York: Norton, 1993.
———. *Sphere: The Form of a Motion*. New York: Norton, 1974.

The Shape of Poetry

In one of his most memorable pronouncements, written in 1917 at a time when he was championing free verse, Ezra Pound made a classic statement about the shape of poetry:

> I think there is a "fluid" as well as a "solid" content, that some poems may have form as a tree has form, some as water poured into a vase. That most symmetrical forms have certain uses. That a vast number of subjects cannot be precisely, and therefore not properly rendered in symmetrical forms.

Written at a time when free verse was a relatively new and exciting development in English-language poetry, Pound's metaphor was a brilliant piece of polemic. While allowing that "symmetrical forms" such as sonnets and villanelles and rhymed quatrains had "certain uses," it suggested that a modern poet would be wise to render most of his subjects in the more flexible, organic form of free verse. A vase might possess a pure, if somewhat abstract and fragile, beauty; but it is, after all, a human artifact—cold and unliving, a relic from the dusty museum of the past. Water poured into it must necessarily conform to its pre-existent shape.

Though Pound's water and vase metaphor was an elegant attempt to resolve the form-content dilemma in formal poetry, it still suggests that the distinction between them is absolute. However perfectly liquid contents and vase seem to meld, water and clay remain distinct, separated by an uncrossable boundary. A tree, by contrast, is a living organism in which form and content are one and the same. The implications of Pound's metaphor are therefore welcomed by poets who write free verse and regarded suspiciously by those who write in traditional forms.

Pound's metaphor has other implications for "symmetrical form" as well, almost all of them negative. For instance, didn't Keats write in a letter to John Taylor: "That if Poetry comes not as naturally as the Leaves to a tree it had better not come at all"? Leaves are the natural outgrowths of trees, but can a leaf grow from a vase?

Looked at that way, Pound's metaphor seems a classic illustration of Coleridge's definition of organic form in his *Lectures on Shakespeare*, where he corrected those critics who confounded "mechanical regularity with organic form":

> The form is mechanic when on any given material we impress a predetermined form, not necessarily arising out of the properties of the material, as when to a mass of wet clay we give whatever shape we wish it to retain when hardened. The organic form, on the other hand, is innate; it shapes as it develops itself from within, and the fulness of its development is one and the same with the perfection of its outward form.

To a modern poet, the act of pouring poetic content into a vase-like "predetermined form" seems every bit as mechanical, and even less original, than pressing clay into a vase. Even considering the sacramental, mystical qualities attributed to water, one can't help thinking of the parable of the wine skins. As a result, writers of free verse from Pound to the present have argued that for poetry to be organic, it must be unbound by the mechanical regularity of meter and the formal rules and strictures of traditional poetry.

Merely looking at the two types of verse on the page seems to confirm Pound's intuition. A passage of the late *Cantos*, or a poem by Charles Olson or A. R. Ammons, sprawls down the page with the scraggly branchiness of an oak tree, or zigzags from margin to margin like tide and shore. The shape of formal verse, on the other hand, is suggestive of lines, planes, squares, and stacked boxes. Its kinship to Pound's vase seems obvious.

A half-century after Pound published his notes on form in "A Retrospect," A. R. Ammons published "Corsons Inlet," a now-classic poetic manifesto, which makes a similar distinction between the organic shapes of nature—and by analogy of free verse—and the more regular symmetries of traditional poetry. In Ammons's poem, the speaker walks among the sand dunes and along the shoreline of Corsons Inlet, watching sand and ocean intermingle, and musing suggestively in words that echo Pound:

> ... I was released from forms,
> from the perpendiculars
>   straight lines, blocks, boxes, binds
> of thought
> into the hues, shadings, rises, flowing bends and blends
>   of sight ...

A few lines later, he makes similar observations:

> ... in nature there are few sharp lines: there are areas of
> primrose
>   more or less dispersed;
> disorderly orders of bayberry; between the rows
> of dunes,
> irregular swamps of reeds ...

A sharp observer of natural detail, Ammons does note that nature has a few symmetrical, vase-like shapes close to hand, but he quickly dismisses their significance, contrasting their small, tight organization with the more sprawling, dynamic forms all around him:

> ... in the smaller view, order tight with shape:
> blue tiny flowers on a leafless weed: carapace of crab:
> snail shell:
>> pulsations of order
>> in the bellies of minnows: orders swallowed,
> broken down, transferred through membranes
> to strengthen larger orders: but in the large view, no
> lines or changeless shapes: the working in and out, together
>> and against, of millions of events: this,
>>> so that I make
>>> no form of
>>> formlessness. ...

Trained in biology, with a bachelor's degree in science from Wake Forest College, Ammons uses the vocabulary of science to elaborate his ideas. For instance, while looking over the sand dunes and clumps of bayberry, he describes the flocking behavior of a group of swallows, using scientific terms such as *chaos* and *entropy*:

>> ... thousands of tree swallows
>> gathering for flight:
>> an order held
>> in constant change: a congregation
> rich with entropy: nevertheless, separable, noticeable
>> as one event,
>>> not chaos ...

Then while still musing on the birds and other "disorderly orders" he's observed around him, Ammons considers "the possibility of rule" in nature "as the sum of rulelessness."

Thirty years have passed since Ammons published "Corsons Inlet," and in that time, discoveries in science and mathematics have shed new light on the problems discussed in his poem—discoveries with immense significance for our understanding of form and content, nature and art, organic and mechanical form. In retrospect, Ammons's use of the phrase "not chaos" in his description of the swallows' behavior is startlingly prescient because, in fact, a whole new science of chaos—or "anti-chaos," as it's sometimes called—has come into being precisely to explain such phenomena. Surprisingly, though, what the new sciences of chaos and complexity have shown is that Ammons is wrong in his conclusions about art and nature: that the "rule" of nature is not the sum of "rulelessness," as he proposes, but is clearly derived from formal rules and principles, which can be described and even imitated by a new form of mathematics called fractal geometry. Thanks to these new discoveries, we now know that the "order tight with shape" he observes in a tiny snail shell is the same order seen in "the large view" in coastlines, weather systems, sand dunes, mountain ranges, and galaxies. That the laws governing the growth of trees—as well as of leaves, ferns, pinecones, and sunflowers—is the same law that governs the growth of human organs, snowflakes, tornadoes, bird wings—and, I will argue, the elegant, broken symmetries of formal verse.

It turns out that writing formal poetry is not at all like pouring water into a vase but, rather, like the growth of a tree—far more so than writing free verse, which, except in special cases, is too ruleless, arbitrary, and mechanical to produce the organic integrity of a good sonnet.

Let's begin by considering those flocking swallows.

In his book *Complexity: The Emerging Science at the Edge of Order and Chaos*, M. Mitchell Waldrop describes a presentation by Craig Reynolds at the Santa Fe Institute on the flocking behavior of birds. As Waldrop explains it, Reynolds placed a number of "autonomous, bird-like agents," which he called "boids," into an artificial environment filled with obstacles on a computer screen. Then to see if flocking behavior could be generated by applying a few simple rules, each boid was programmed to behave in the following ways:

1. to maintain a minimum distance from other objects in the environment, including other boids;
2. to match velocities with boids in its neighborhood;
3. to move toward a perceived center of mass of boids in its neighborhood.

Waldrop describes the results of this computer simulation as follows:

What was striking about these rules was that none of them said, "Form a flock." Quite the opposite: the rules were entirely local, referring only to what an individual boid could see and do in its own vicinity. If a flock was going to form at all, it would have to do so from the bottom up, as an emergent phenomenon. And yet flocks *did* form, every time. Reynolds could start his simulation with boids scattered around the computer screen completely at random, and they could spontaneously collect themselves into a flock that could fly around obstacles in a very fluid and natural manner. Sometimes the flock would even break into subflocks that flowed around both sides of an obstacle, rejoining on the other side as if the boids had planned it all along.

One of the most interesting aspects of the emergent behavior of the flock of "boids" noted by Waldrop was that there was no top-down rule telling the boids to form flocks: "Instead of writing global, top-down specifications for how the flock should behave or telling his creatures to follow the lead of a Boss Boid, Reynolds had used only the three simple rules of local, boid-to-boid interaction."

This should alleviate the fears of those poets who, like Ammons, think that by writing in traditional forms they are submitting their work to the arbitrary rule of authority, to the top-down rules and "Boss Boids" of the past. In "Corsons Inlet," Ammons explicitly rejects such authority, arguing that in poetry, as in nature, there is, or should be,

> no arranged terror: no forcing of image, plan,
> or thought:
> no propaganda, no humbling of reality to precept. . . .

Ironically, though, by rejecting the rules of formal poetry, Ammons is not, as he declares in the poem, leaving "all possibilities / of escape open" but rather cutting himself off from the possibility of achieving the types of rule-governed behavior that produce nature's emergent forms. Once we look at how poems actually take shape, it becomes clear that Ammons and Pound are wrong: The rules of formal poetry generate not static objects like vases, but the same kind of bottom-up, self-organizing processes seen in complex natural systems such as flocking birds, shifting sand dunes, and living trees.

Richard Wilbur, perhaps the foremost living practitioner of traditional verse in America, described in a recent interview (*The Formalist*) what happens when he starts to write:

> . . . my practice is absolutely the reverse of saying, well, let's write a sestina now, let's see if I can write a rondeau. I've never, never found myself doing that kind of thing. It's always a matter of sensing that something wants to be said, something of which, as yet, I have a very imperfect knowledge, and letting it start to talk, and finding what rhythm it wants to come out in, what phrasing seems natural to it. When I've discovered those things for a couple of lines, I begin to have the stanza of my poem, if I'm going to have a stanzaic poem. In any case, the line lengths declare themselves organically as they do, I suppose, for a free verse poet. The difference between me and a free verse poet is simply that I commit myself to the metrical precedents which my first lines set. I have found that though I don't know how a poem is going to end, I always have a pretty good advance awareness of how long the poem is going to be, what its tone is going to be, and thus can initially arrive at rhythms and line lengths which are going to be capable of repetition without troubling the flow of thought as it emerges.

The process Wilbur describes will, I'm sure, sound familiar to other writers of formal poetry. It also echoes what scientists who work with chaotic and complex systems describe as happening in nature. John Briggs, for instance, in his book *Fractals: The Patterns of Chaos*, describes what happens when silicon oil is heated to a boil in a container. At first, as the heat is applied, the oil merely roils and bubbles chaotically in random turbulence; then suddenly, a startlingly complex and intricate pattern emerges:

> As soon as the temperature difference between the bottom and the top of the container reaches a critical point, the convection cells bubbling chaotically from the boundaries of the container self-organize themselves so that a symmetry hidden in the chaos asserts itself.

The photograph accompanying his description shows a beautiful pattern of hexagonal convection cells, packed together like the beeswax cells of a honeycomb. The sudden appearance of this beautiful geometrical arrangement is completely unpredictable and results from nature's surprising ability to self-organize holistically, through a complex and sensitive system of feedback, into an emergent new form. As Wilbur describes it, the way a mass of bubbling chaotic thoughts and scattered phrases turns into a sonnet or villanelle is very similar to the seemingly magical transformation that occurs in heated silicon oil. Writing a sonnet, it turns out, is less like pouring water into a dead clay mold than like heating water and watching it suddenly self-organize into a vase.

The term scientists now use to describe the complex, elegant patterns that emerge from nonlinear dynamic systems is "strange attractor." The honeycomb pattern emerging from heated silicon oil is one; a tornado organizing itself from random atmospheric turbulence is another. Completely unpredictable from the behavior of its constituent parts, a strange attractor is a higher-order, emergent phenomenon. Like the flocking behavior of real birds and computer "boids," it somehow spontaneously happens when a simple set of rules, interacting in a holistic way throughout a complex system, produces a dynamic new form of order.

There's a deep paradox here, and one that poets should pause to consider. On the one hand, a poem in its early stages resembles the chaotic random activity of a storm, organizing itself through a rule-governed process of self-adjustment and feedback to produce the strange attractor: the poem. On the other hand, as its name suggests, the *attractor*—the finished poem—somehow *draws* the turbulence into its final shape. It's both a top-down and a bottom-up phenomena—what Douglas Hofstadter calls a "strange loop" or "tangled hierarchy."

From the testimony of Richard Wilbur and other poets, it appears that a poem begins with "something that wants to be said," which generates random phrases and rhythms that organize themselves into lines, then shapely stanzas, then poems. Wilbur says he doesn't decide ahead of time what the line lengths will be but, rather, that they "declare themselves organically." Yet, paradoxically, these initial lines declare themselves into the right lengths because of his dim initial awareness of "how long" and of what the overall "tone" of the poem is going to be. The initial lines determine the shape of the finished poem, yet the overall shape and tone of the finished poem is what draws the initial lines into being.

Donald Hall, in a recent interview *(Poets & Writers)*, gives a similar description of the way poems evolve, declaring that he begins with "a notion of a subject area, maybe a tone of feeling in connection with a phrase, maybe an image with a compelling cadence." He adds that he doesn't know where he's heading with the poem, but simply jots down phrases, often over a period of years, till a sufficient number have accumulated. "The scattered words that accumulate before I start to write," he concludes, "are the first draft of the poem. Along with them I have something like an *impetus* toward a poem, a shadow that hulks toward the page."

Hall's description almost exactly echoes Wilbur's: a poem begins with a mysterious "impetus," a chaotic scattering of rhythms and phrases, and a sense of the poem's overall tone. All of these disparate elements then somehow coalesce into the poem's final form, which also somehow already existed as a strange attractor: "a shadow that hulks toward the page."

The great Argentinean poet Jorge Luis Borges, in his poem "A Poet of the Thirteenth Century," offers a further parallel to the descriptions of Wilbur and Hall. Borges describes how an unnamed thirteenth-century Italian poet (possibly Guittone D'Arezzo) invented the sonnet form in words that suggest the theories of complexity science. As translated by William Ferguson, the poem reads as follows:

Think of him laboring in the Tuscan halls
On the first sonnet (that word still unsaid),
The undistinguished pages, filled with sad
Triplets and quatrains, without heads or tails.

Slowly he shapes it; yet the impulse fails.
He stops, perhaps at a strange slight music shed
From time coming and its holy dread,
A murmuring of far-off nightingales.

Did he sense that others were to follow,
That the arcane, incredible Apollo
Had revealed an archetypal thing,

A whirlpool mirror that would draw and hold
All that night could hide or day unfold:
Daedalus, labyrinth, riddle, Oedipus King?

Borges suggests that the sonnet was an "archetypal thing," a strange attractor that somehow caused those first quatrains and triplets to self-organize by reaching back through time: "... a strange slight music shed / From time coming and its holy dread / A murmuring of far-off nightingales." Borges's final image of an "avid crystal"—or "whirlpool mirror" in Ferguson's translation—is another apt description of the "strange attractor" that pulled myth, riddle, paradox, and labyrinth into the sonnet's equally tangled form.

Still, I know that while some people can accept that the free-flowing forms of leaves and trees are produced by rule-governed natural processes, they cannot believe there's anything natural about poems being coaxed into existence by metrical rules and formal procedures. Coleridge, however, in the same essay quoted above, has already answered those skeptics:

> The spirit of poetry, like all other living powers, must of necessity circumscribe itself by rules, were it only to unite power with beauty. It must embody in order to reveal itself; but a living body is of necessity an organized one—and what is organization but the connection of parts to a whole, so that each part is at once end and means! This is no discovery of criticism; it is a necessity of the human mind—and all nations have felt and obeyed it, in the invention of meter and measured sounds as the vehicle and involucrum of poetry, itself a fellow growth from the same life, even as the bark is to the tree.

As with the poem by Borges, this passage remarkably evokes the discoveries of chaos science. In it, Coleridge declares that as with a living body, "the spirit of poetry" must operate through "rules," which allow a new type of organization incorporating a bottom-up and top-down connection between whole and parts—the way the root system, leaves, bark, and other subsystems of a plant emerge into the thing we call an oak tree. Far from being a dead "received form," meter is, in Coleridge's words, nothing less than the "vehicle and involucrum of poetry," an "involucrum" being the outer covering of part of a plant.

The relationship, therefore, of the "spirit" of poetry to "meter and measured sounds" is not that of water poured into a vase, but, in the words of Coleridge again, "a fellow growth from the same life, even as the bark is to the tree."

The error made by Pound and Ammons is a common one. Like many a contemporary theorist, they saw the shapes that formal poems make on the page, noted their resemblance to Euclidean squares and rectangles, and concluded that they were produced by a different geometry than that which produces the biomorphic shapes of trees and leaves. They mistook the two-dimensional outline of the poem on the page for the shape of the poem itself—which, as Pound said more wisely in another famous aphorism, is a shape cut "into time." In confusing a poem's two-dimensional outline with the four-dimensional shape it creates when spoken or read, poets like Pound and Ammons resemble the citizens of Flatland in the classic novel who see only a two-dimensional cross-section of a multi-dimensional object when it intersects the flat plane of their universe. Like his predecessor Charles Olson, who also composed on a typewriter and thought in spatial terms, Ammons tries to substitute a typewriter's mechanical spacing for the organic coherence produced by rules and "measured sounds." Ammons once even composed an entire book-length poem, *Tape for the Turn of the Year*, on a roll of adding-machine tape, letting its narrow dimensions mechanically dictate the form and rhythms of his poem.

Now, thanks to a new tool, the computer, and a new type of mathematics, fractal geometry, we know that time plays a role in the evolution of nonlinear dynamic systems. We can express the rules governing complex natural systems such as sand dunes and coastlines and measure their shapes in precise mathematical ways. Using fractal geometry, we can even assign a shape like a coastline a fractal dimension. (The coast of England, for example, has a fractal dimension of 1.25.) We now know that the shapes of trees and leaves are not the sums of "rulelessness," as Ammons proposed, but the result of a rule-governed process dictated by their DNA and feedback from the environment as they adjust themselves in an endless feedback loop.

Like growing leaves and changing coastlines, the nonlinear equations of fractal geometry need time to enact their iterations. Unlike linear equations, which simply plug numbers in and calculate the answer to a result, nonlinear equations feed the results of each step back into themselves, altering themselves and their outcome through constant feedback, and thus creating a perfect mathematical analog to the processes undergone by living things.

For instance, one of the simplest types of nonlinear equations is the Fibonacci sequence. Starting with the number 1, the sequence then progresses to 1, 2, 3, 5, 8, 13, 21, 34, so that each number is the sum of the two preceding it. The approximate ratio of each number to the preceding one is .618, the number of the golden section. The poet John Frederick Nims, in his book *Western Wind*, finds this ratio in the proportions of the golden rectangle, and demonstrates how when the golden rectangle is subdivided into smaller and smaller versions of itself and connected by a curving line through corresponding points, it produces the spiral found in a nautilus shell—one of those small forms "tight with shape" Ammons mentioned in "Corsons Inlet." The same golden section ratio can also be found in other natural objects such as the spiral of sunflowers and the curve of mountain goat horns.

Nims has even speculated that the ratio in the golden section might lie behind the proportions of the Petrarchan sonnet, giving further support to Borges' suggestion that the sonnet is an "archetypal thing" discovered by a Tuscan poet in the thirteenth century. Interestingly, the Fibonacci sequence was discovered by another thirteenth-century Italian, Filius Bonacci.

But the perfect symmetry of the nautilus shell is clearly of a different type than that of leaves and trees, not to mention clouds and coastlines. That's because the nonlinear equation that produces the Fibonacci sequence lacks the element of chance provided by environmental feedback to a tree or a boulder-strewn beach. But as John Briggs and F. David Peat note in their book *Turbulent Mirror*, "When a random variation in the iterations is allowed so that details vary from scale to scale, it's possible to mimic the actual forms and structures of nature much more closely. This suggests natural growth is produced through a combination of iteration and chance." They go on to show that by "combining an iterative scaling with a random element of choice," the shapes of mountains and coastlines can be generated so realistically on computers that they're now used in movies and videos. A landscape similar to Corsons Inlet can now be generated on a computer screen.

Fractal scaling, another element common to both natural forms and fractal geometry, is the tendency of a fractal shape to be self-similar at various scales. For instance, the shape of a coastline remains the same no matter what the distance of the observer, whether he's a passenger on a jet, a mountain climber, a beach stroller, or child with a magnifying glass. Biomorphic shapes such as trees and leaves also display self-similarity at different scales: it's found in the fractal branching of limbs and twigs and in the vascular branching of its leaves. Another thing that causes the symmetry of natural forms to be irregular is the fact that some incorporate several fractal scales in their designs. For instance, human lungs have one fractal dimension for the first twenty branches, then a different scale after that.

As we've seen, the shape of a living thing such as a leaf is produced when the instructions coded in its DNA encounter chance elements such as wind, sun, heat, cold, and disease. Using a similar combination of coded rules and random elements, a mathematician named Michael Barnsley has invented a way to create remarkably leaf-like structures through a process he calls "affine transformations." As Briggs and Peat describe it, the process begins by shrinking and skewing the picture of a full-size leaf into "a smaller distorted version of the original. The affine idea is to find several of these smaller leaf transformations that can be overlapped into a collage that has the shape of the original full-size leaf." After shingling several of these small distorted versions of the leaf together, Barnsley starts at a point on a computer and, "using his affine transformations and iteration, . . . generates a fractal attractor that looks like the original leaf." Using a similar method (Barnsley calls it "collage theorem"), he has also created various computer-generated shapes of living ferns.

The poet Gerard Manley Hopkins, another astute observer of nature, seems to have discovered the "collage theorem" on his own more than a hundred years before Barnsley. In his journal entry of July 19, 1866, Hopkins describes what sounds awfully like the "affine transformations" for an oak leaf when he writes: "I have now found the law of oak leaves. It is of platter-shaped stars altogether." Hopkins also seems aware of other shaping principles in nature such as self-similarity and fractal scaling. Writing in his journal again (July 25, 1868), he compares the shapes of clouds to patterns seen in fungus: "From the summit the view on the Italian side was broken by endless ranges of part-vertical dancing cloud, the highest and furthest flaked and foiled like fungus and colored pink." Benoit Mandelbrot, the inventor of fractal geometry, in his rhapsodic description of the fractal shapes of nature, practically echoes Hopkins's poem "Pied Beauty" when he writes of the "grainy, hydralike, in between, pimply, pocky, ramified, sea-weedy, strange, tangled, tortuous, wiggly, whispy, wrinkled" shapes that can now "be approached in rigorous and vigorous fashion" through his fractal geometry. If we substitute the assonantally chiming word *fractal* for *dappled* in the first line of Hopkins' poem ("Glory be to God for *fractal* things"), its celebration of all that's "fickle, freckled (who knows how?)" sounds, in turn, remarkably like Mandelbrot.

What we are beginning to see, I hope, is that the laws governing the evolution of living and other natural forms are the same laws that govern the creation of poetry. So let's summarize what these laws are and show how they apply.

First, symmetrical forms such as sonnets, villanelles, and ballad stanzas are not static "received forms"; they evolve, like plants, through a process of iteration and feedback. The regular meter of formal poets is not a dull mechanical ticking, like a clock's; it coalesces out of the rhythms of randomly jotted phrases through a process of "phase-locking"—a natural process that occurs, in the words of Briggs and Peat again, "when many individual oscillators shift from a state of collective chaos to beating together or resonating in harmony." As two examples, they describe the way the randomly flickering lights of fireflies become synchronous throughout a whole tree, and the way the menstrual cycles of women living in close proximity often phase-lock into a single, collective rhythm.

Ralph Waldo Emerson, no champion of either conformity or mechanical regularity, has also suggested that meter and poetic form are inextricably tangled in an organic unity, writing, "It is not meters, but a meter-making argument that makes a poem,—a thought so passionate and alive that like the spirit of a plant or an animal it has an architecture of its own"; a thought echoed by Whitman, who writes, "The rhyme and uniformity of perfect poems show the free growth of metrical laws and bud from them as unerringly and loosely as lilacs or roses on a bush, and take shapes as compact as the shapes of chestnuts and oranges and melons and pears, and shed the perfume of impalpable form."

Regular meter is also a source of feedback, another element of organic form. Once the random phrases and rhythms in a poet's scattered fragments begin to phase-lock into a recognizable meter, every subsequent line must take a similar form. During the composition of a metrical poem, the poet is often forced to rearrange and substitute words till the meter feels right. And when the meter begins to feel too regular, he will allow some random variations to occur, or consciously add substitutions, to reshape a line.

Rhyme is another attribute of formal poetry that increases feedback by forcing the poet to listen to what she writes. Each time it sends a poet to her rhyming dictionary, it adds an element of randomness— the way weather influences the growth of a tree. To fit the new rhyme into her scheme, the poet often has to invent new metaphors and introduce new ideas, thus altering the course of the entire poem. Furthermore, once the rhyme-scheme becomes clear to the poet in the early lines, it affects the development and arrangement of every future line as the poem evolves toward its final form.

In addition, rhyme prevents a poem from being merely a linear succession of so-called "breath units" scored on a two-dimensional plane. By reaching back to earlier rhymes and forward to future rhymes, each new rhyme twists the entire poem back on itself in a self-interfering knot.

A formal poem is also holistic. One alteration in a line's meter or rhyme scheme affects the writing, interpretation, and affective value of every other line.

The self-similarity of fractal scaling is another element shared by formal poetry, natural forms, and fractal geometry. We can see it in the scaled, fractal branching of the human circulatory system and in the identical paisley patterns seen at different scales of a purely mathematical object like the Mandelbrot set. The same self-similarity and scaling occur in formal poetry. Frederick Turner has found what might be the most remarkable use of self-similarity in all of literature in Dante's *Divine Comedy*, in which, Turner writes, "the three-line stanza of its microcosm is echoed in the trinitarian theology of its middle-level organization and in the tripartite structure of the whole poem." Narrative poems such as the *Divine Comedy* and the *Aeneid* of Dante's master, Virgil, offer additional levels of fractal scaling as episode branches into episode, creating eddies and turbulence that both contribute to and resemble the larger narrative movements of the poem.

The reason natural forms such as trees and leaves rarely display the perfect symmetry of a nautilus shell or the Mandelbrot set is that their forms possess what scientists call "broken symmetry," also described as "similarity with a difference." Here again, we can find a parallel in formal poetry, wherein no two metrical lines are ever identical. Metrical substitutions are one source of asymmetry; but even when no variations occur, subtle differences of stress and duration will make any two lines as different as two snowflakes. There is also a symmetry-breaking tension in the subtle differences between a line's abstract metrical pattern and the speech rhythms playing against it. Rhyme is yet another source of "similarity with a difference," since by definition it's produced by words compounded of both similar and dissimilar sounds.

Finally, we must consider the emergent features that appear in all kinds of dynamic nonlinear systems, from trees to poems. One such emergent feature is beauty. Though Joyce Kilmer claims never to have seen "a poem lovely as a tree," others have found in poems an equal, or surpassing, beauty. Poems not only share the wild, inexplicably beautiful proportions of natural forms, they also engage our minds and perceptions at higher levels, mirroring our moral and intellectual complexities. They have the power to move and transform us.

Consider the following poem by Charles Martin, which illustrates much of the above.

METAPHOR OF GRASS IN CALIFORNIA

The seeds of certain grasses that once grew
Over the graves of those who fell at Troy
Were brought to California in the hooves
Of Spanish cattle. Trodden into the soil,

They liked it well enough to germinate,
Awakening into another scene
Of conquest: blade fell upon flashing blade
Until the native grasses fled the field,

And the native flowers bowed to their dominion.
Small clumps of them fought on as they retreated
Toward isolated ledges of serpentine,
Repellent to their conquerors. . . .
                                    In defeat,
They were like men who see their city taken,
And think of grass—how soon it will conceal
All of the scattered bodies of the slain;
As such men fall, these fell, but silently.

The poem opens with two lines of carefully interwoven vowels and consonants, alliterating "seeds" and "certain"; "grass," "grew," and "graves." This interlocking mesh of sounds is echoed at higher levels in the metrical rhythms holding individual lines together and binding all of them into a collective unity; it's repeated again in the four strenuously discordant off-rhymes that lock each quatrain into place and make each stanza resemble the others in form and structure.

The first stanza introduces the extended metaphor that will be elaborated throughout the rest of the poem, telling how the seeds of grasses that once grew "Over the graves of those who fell at Troy" were introduced into the New World. By using his metaphor of grass, the poet is able to show not only similarities between the conquest of Troy by Greeks and New World natives by Europeans, but to echo both conquests at a lower level in the war between species of grass. The metaphor enables the poet to set all the historical events against the much vaster scale of evolutionary time, with its vast cyclic movements of Darwinian struggle, adaptation, and mass extinction.

With each stanza, the metaphor complexifies and deepens, so that by the time the poem describes the native flowers bowing to the "dominion" of the new grasses and retreating toward "ledges of serpentine," we can't help but think of the devastation and gradual retreat of Native Americans into those badlands called reservations. The chilling similarities evoked by the metaphor are echoed in the violent chiming of the poem's off-rhymes as well as in the regularly repeating rhythms of its meter. As the poem expands, its large-scale metaphoric and thematic similarities are mirrored all the way down to the level of individual words as the poet writes punningly of how "blade fell upon flashing blade," where sword and grass, men and nature, are reflected in a single monosyllable.

After the personification of the earlier stanzas, the final stanza comes as a shock. Speaking of the defeated native grasses, the poem declares, "They were like men who see their city taken, / And think of grass—how soon it will conceal / All of the scattered bodies of the slain," thus creating a tangled loop reminiscent of M. C. Escher: the native grasses are like men who, in defeat, think of how grass will cover their dead (human) bodies. A further tangling of levels occurs when we consider the food chain the poet secrets into the poem: the grass seeds arrive in the hooves of cattle; cattle eat grass; men eat cattle; when men die, they are eaten by grass, which is eaten by cattle; and so on to infinity.

Switching from the implicit comparison of metaphor to the explicit comparison of simile ("They were *like* men who see their city taken" [italics mine]), the poet is able to spring a sudden reversal in the poem's last line: "As such men fall, these fell, but silently." That final "similarity with a difference" delivers the poem's moral shock. *Yes*, we think, grasses are *like* men, but they fall *silently*—without tragedy or conscious suffering, in a world devoid of moral responsibility. In that difference lies a whole universe, filled with all the horror and tragic beauty of our lives. Martin's deceptively simple sixteen-line poem captures an almost infinitely complex set of nested scales—from the lowest, sensual level of patterned sounds up to the highest level of ethical and moral feelings.

Perhaps no poet, mathematician, or scientist of the last two hundred years has understood the laws of creation better—or embodied them more brilliantly—then Gerard Manley Hopkins. From his readings in the Medieval philosopher Duns Scotus, his own first-hand observations of nature, and his reflections on poetic form, Hopkins synthesized a surprisingly accurate theory of organic form. Consider the following extract from his journal dated February 24, 1875:

> In the snow flat-topped hillocks and shoulders outlined with wavy edges, ridge below ridge, very like the grain of wood in line and in projection like relief maps. These the wind makes I think and of course drifts, which are in fact snow waves. The sharp nape of a drift is sometimes broken by slant flutes or channels. I think this must be when the wind after shaping the drift first has changed and cast waves in the body of the wave itself. All the world is full of inscape and chance left free to act falls into an order as well as purpose: looking out of my window I caught it in the random clods and broken heaps of snow made by the cast of a broom.

Not only does Hopkins see the similarity between snow drifts and waves, he also notes that the pattern of their "wavy edges" is similar to the grain pattern in wood and to another fractal pattern: hills on a relief map. Hopkins sees nature's fractal scaling in the smaller waves etched into the larger drifts. Then he makes the most astounding observation of all, defining the principle underlying all such patterns when he writes, "All the world is full of inscape *and chance left free to act falls into an order* as well as a purpose" (italics mine). A modern chaosologist couldn't have said it better. Chance, left free to act, will fall into an order. Hopkins notes the same order in "the random clods and broken heaps of snow made by the cast of a broom."

This is not to say that Hopkins believed that the intricate forms of nature are produced by chance alone, or that poetry can be written by giving rein to ungoverned impulses. He believed that natural forms are produced by chance combined with natural law, and spent his whole life working out an elaborate system to explain the patterns he descried in art and nature. The word "inscape," which he used in the passage above, was Hopkins's term for the inner design or pattern that causes an object's distinctive shape; he applied the term to a surprisingly wide range of phenomena, from music, paintings, and poems to trees, clouds, and waterfalls. He also meant the term to suggest something like what Duns Scotus called *haecceitas*, the individualizing *thisness* found in everything in nature. Hopkins coined another word, *instress*, to define the force that upholds an object's inscape. He believed that even the most seemingly random patterns in nature are produced by instress and can therefore be perceived, understood, and artistically rendered. For instance, in a journal entry dated August 10, 1872, he describes the patterns made by withdrawing waves on sand and notes how the eyes "unpack the huddling and gnarls of the water and *law out* the shapes and the sequence of the running" (italics mine).

Hopkins also believed it was possible for a reader to "law out" a poem's inscape. In fact, in some early lecture notes, he described poetry as "speech only employed to carry the inscape of speech for the inscape's sake." In a letter to his friend Robert Bridges, he rebukes poets like Ammons and Olson who ignore a poem's inscape by reading only with their eyes, telling his correspondent not to read his poems "with the eyes but with [his] ears."

Anticipating the work of Frederick Turner, a synthesizing genius of our own time, Hopkins insisted that all the arts, including poetry, had to be performed to be fully experienced. In a letter to his brother Everard (November 1885), the poet stated that "every work of art has its own play or performance." And after defining how drama, symphonic music, and painting each achieves its performance, Hopkins added, "A house performs when it is now built and lived in. To come nearer: books play, perform, or are played and performed when they are read."

A final poem by Hopkins will illustrate the depth of his understanding and achievement. Published without a title, it is known by its first line.

As kingfishers catch fire, dragonflies draw flame;
As tumbled over rim in roundy wells
Stones ring; like each tucked string tells, each hung bell's
Bow swung finds tongue to fling out broad its name;
Each mortal thing does one thing and the same:
Deals out that being indoors each one dwells;
Selves—goes itself; *myself* it speaks and spells,
Crying *What I do is me: for that I came.*

I say more: the just man justices;
Keeps grace: that keeps all his goings graces;
Acts in God's eye what in God's eye he is—
Christ. For Christ plays in ten thousand places,
Lovely in limbs, and lovely in eyes not his
To the Father through the features of men's faces.

By now, we hardly need to point out how the poem performs itself, joining its various elements in one organic wholeness. We might
begin by noting that it's a Petrarchan sonnet, then observe how the
rhyming of the sestet, *cdcdcd*, contrasts with the envelope rhyme
scheme of the octave—like the shift from one fractal dimension to
another in the branching of human lungs. We might also note how
the poem's end-rhymes are echoed in rhymes and thick clusters of
assonantally chiming sounds within the lines, and how the lush as-
sonance of the poem finds a parallel in its dense alliteration. Taken
together, there's not a more densely interwoven texture of sound in
English poetry.

But the rhyming doesn't stop at the level of sound: Hopkins also
"rhymes" on the higher level of metaphor, first in the flashing of
kingfisher and dragonfly, then in the following lines where he rhymes
the sounds of stones falling into wells with plucked strings and rung
bells. Rhyming sense with sense, he also makes flashing kingfisher
rhyme with vibrating strings and bells as each thing deals out "that
being indoors each one dwells."

The entire poem celebrates a self-similarity that extends throughout creation, from the distinctive beauty of pebbles and insects, to

the higher forms of ethical and moral beauty in people, up to the very highest informing beauty of the creator himself. According to Hopkins, everything from a dragonfly to God not only possesses a distinctive beauty, a special *thisness*, it *selves*—a verb, notice, not a noun. This selving is a living process that happens across all levels of being; it is a lived *performance*. Hopkins declares that the just man "*Acts* in God's eye what in God's eye he is"; that "Christ *plays* in ten thousand places" (italics mine). Everything in creation—from "selving" pebbles and dragonflies to the man who "justices" and "keeps all his goings graces"—is tangled in one self-interfering loop. In man, the creative principle—what Hopkins calls God—achieves a transformative self-consciousness, able to act "in God's eye what in God's eye [it] is." A man is not only nature observing itself, but embodied personhood (like the incarnate Christ); he is God observing Himself. The final three lines of the poem capture this self-reflexive, paradoxical entangledness with remarkable beauty and economy: "For Christ plays in ten thousand places, / Lovely in limbs, and lovely in eyes not his / To the Father through the features of men's faces." Christ plays *to* the creator, who is also paradoxically himself, through the "features of men's faces," with their distinctive, character-revealing symmetries and fractal wrinkles.

Hopkins enacts his own selving in this poem in part through his distinctive style, nowhere more clearly than in his first line, where he plays out the implications of his metaphor at every level of sound, syntax, and rhythm:

As kingfishers catch fire, dragonflies draw flame. . . .

The pattern of *k* and *f* sounds in the first half of the line is exactly duplicated in the interlocking pattern of *dr* and *f* sounds in the second. Running through this pattern of alliteration and binding it together is the assonantal chiming of short *a* sounds in "as," "catch," and "dragon." The syntax and rhythm of the two halves of the line are also nearly identical:

As kingfishers catch fire, dragonflies draw flame. . . .

A slight asymmetry is caused by the extra unstressed syllable of "As" and the ghostly extra syllable hovering at the end of *fire* in the first half of the line, as well as by subtle differences in the stress and duration of corresponding syllables in each.

A further asymmetry lies in the way the first line departs from the dominant iambic pattern of the poem. This asymmetry appears again most noticeably in the poem's last line, which hovers suspended between three almost equally plausible scansions of its rhythms. The line can be heard as extremely loose iambic pentameter, with an anapestic substitution in the first foot, an iamb with a courtesy accent on "through" in the second, a normal iamb in the third, and a pyrrhic and spondee (with a feminine ending) in the last two; as trochaic hexameter, with five of its six feet falling; and as an oddly symmetrical three-stress line composed of three anapests, with an extra unstressed syllable after each. The alliteration of the three heavily stressed syllables in "Father," "features," and "faces" lends additional weight to this reading.

Given Hopkins's experiments with accentual verse, one might argue that this poem's metrical irregularities are due to its use of "sprung rhythm," an accentual pattern, usually with five stresses per line, developed by the poet from his readings in Anglo-Saxon verse. But the poem's second line is so perfectly iambic that it establishes a clear metrical paradigm, retroactively influencing the way we see the first, which can be scanned as above, with an iamb, pyrrhic, and spondee before the comma; and "headless" iamb, pyrrhic, and spondee after. Though this particular arrangement bears the inscape of Hopkins's peculiar genius, the use of pyrrhic and spondee is common in iambic verse. Matthew Arnold, for instance, uses it in "Dover Beach" to create a line similar to that of Hopkins: "Come to the window, sweet is the night air."

A similar situation arises in the final line, where, in order to get our five stresses, we have to count either the lightly stressed "To" or "through," as well as "men's"—though none receives anywhere near the weight of the stresses in *Fathers, features, faces*. Within the larger metrical context, however, we can scan the line as above, as loose iambic. If we regard each line as a gestalt, even some of Hopkins's most difficult lines can be scanned as iambic pentameter—though a pentameter with a higher than usual number of stresses due to his frequent spondaic substitutions.

All of which goes to show how holistic a formal poem is, how every line and every individual foot within it affects the reading of every other line and syllable. Though Hopkins substitutes with unparalleled boldness, especially in the sestet, where the lines buckle and strain against the iambic matrix, we have only to compare this poem to others such as "Spelt from Sibyl's Leaves" or "Carrion Comfort" (both experimental "sonnets" with the same rhyme scheme) to see the difference between it and the poet's more thoroughgoing experiments in sprung rhythm.

In "As kingfishers catch fire," it seems that the sonnet form itself (that archetypal thing) reaches down to influence the reading of each constituent part by awakening expectations in us for certain rhymes and rhythms. Every fragment of syntax, every complication of metaphor influences every other part of the poem in ways both large and small. It is difficult to conceive how a poem without the regularly recurring rhythms or self-repeating forms of Hopkins's sonnet could produce such complexity of design or richness of interpretation.

Through parallelisms of syntax and similarities of metaphors and sounds, free verse can sometimes attain isolated expressions of self-similarity in its parts and approximation of order in its overall design; but with fewer rules and less feedback to amplify and vary its constituent elements, it generally fails to achieve the same degree of self-similarity and scaling we find in the best formal verse. Drawn into being not so much by a strange attractor as by a series of provisional judgments and mechanical operations such as hitting return and space keys on a keyboard, free verse can only imitate the most superficial aspects of living forms like trees. Hopkins, even as a young man, suggested as much in an undergraduate essay on "Poetic Diction":

> The structure of poetry is that of continuous parallelism, ranging from the technical so-called Parallelisms of Hebrew poetry and the antiphons of Church music up to the intricacy of Greek or Italian or English verse.

Suggesting that there's a hierarchy of forms in poetry and music, Hopkins calls the "so-called Parallelisms" of free verse *technical* in nature and denies even the Hebrew poetry of the Bible the organic "intricacy" of classical forms.

Science and Poetry

A View from the Divide

The most remarkable discovery made by scientists is science itself. The discovery must be compared in importance with the invention of cave-painting and writing. Like these earlier human creations, science is an attempt to control our surroundings by entering into them and understanding them from inside. And like them, science has surely made a critical step in human development and cannot be reversed.—Jacob Bronowski

The great English poet John Donne published *An Anatomy of the World* in 1611, one year after Galileo's first accounts of his work with the telescope appeared. The poem was probably commissioned as a funeral elegy for Elizabeth Drury, who died at age fourteen, the daughter of a wealthy London landowner. But that loss is not the only spiritual dislocation the poem commemorates. The universe suddenly had been peppered with ten times the stars that had been there before. The perception of the Earth's place in that expanded (though not yet expanding) universe had been thrown into metaphysical revolution. Donne was not convinced by the new theories of Copernicus and Brahe placing the sun at the center and the Earth as merely a whirling outlier, but he took them seriously enough that one can feel his inner sense reeling:

And new philosophy calls all in doubt,
The element of fire is quite put out;
The sun is lost, and th' earth, and no man's wit
Can well direct him where to look for it.
And freely men confess that this world's spent,
When in the planets, and the firmament
They seek so many new . . .
'Tis all in pieces, all coherence gone. . . .

Part of his task as a poet was to integrate this new information about the nature of reality with his beliefs and emotions, to give a voice to his very process of confusion, his struggle for equilibrium in a newly unstable world. It is difficult to imagine a conceptual change more profound than the one experienced during the first century of modern science. The Copernican revolution meant that people could no longer trust their senses. The experience of observing the sun circle around the Earth, as one might continue to witness every day, was no longer the truth. What then could be the value of the senses, of experience, after one has learned that the truth requires tests, measurement, and collective scrutiny?

That shift in earthlings' fundamental sense of place may not seem like a big deal now. We have had a few centuries to get used to living with its psychic disjunction. But science (along with its headstrong, profiteering offspring, technology) has not slowed down in presenting artists with destabilizing new realities. As we pass the millennium, the dizzying changes in chaos and quantum and genome theories, in the neurophysics of the brain and the biotechnology of reproduction, and in the search for the Theory of Everything can send the amateur science watcher into a state of permanent vertigo. Indeed, I am surprised at how few contemporary artists, and in particular poets, have captured that sense of reeling. Certainly there are some—A. R. Ammons, Richard Kenney, Pattiann Rogers, James Merrill,

Diane Ackerman, Miroslav Holub, May Swenson, Jorie Graham, and Loren Eiseley all have made footholds in the shifting terrain.

Nevertheless, the view from either side of the disciplinary divide seems to be that poetry and science are fundamentally opposed, if not hostile to one another. Scientists are seekers of fact; poets revelers in sensation. Scientists seek a clear, verifiable, and elegant theory; contemporary poets, as critic Helen Vendler recently put it, create objects that are less and less like well-wrought urns, and more and more like the misty collisions and diffusions that take place in a cloud chamber. The popular view demonizes us both, perhaps because we serve neither the god of profit-making nor the god of usefulness. Scientists are the cold-hearted dissectors of all that is beautiful; poets the lunatic heirs to pagan forces. We are made to embody the mythic split in Western civilization between the head and the heart. But none of this divided thinking rings true to my experience as a poet.

In my high-school biology notebook, which I keep with the few artifacts of my youth that continue to interest me, among the drawings in meticulous colored pencil of the life cycles of diploblastic coelenterata and hermaphroditic annelids, is a simple schematic of an unspecified point in human history at which science and religion took separate paths as ways to understand the world. I still can picture my biology teacher with his waxy crewcut and a sport jacket standing at the blackboard explaining the schism as simply as if it were an intersection on a highway. What could be tested and measured took the road of science, he said, and the unknown took the other. It is the drawing I remember most keenly because it seemed to me, even then, puzzling. How could the great questions about the nature of existence be separated into subjects, professions, vocabularies that had little to say to one another? Wasn't everyone, wasn't all knowledge and ignorance, joined by the simple desire to know the physical world, to learn how "I" got to be a part of it and to make some meaning out of our collective existence? How would the world look, I wondered, if one could see it from a point prior to that split?

I was hooked. Science became for me, not the precinct of facts, but the place where the most interesting questions were asked. I knew that no matter how much the professional rigor of science demanded objectivity, there would always be the curiosity and bewilderment of a human being hiding somewhere in the data. And though decades would pass before I heard the name Heisenberg, I already began to sense what I would later read: "Even in science the object of research is no longer nature itself, but man's investigation of nature."

That year for the school science fair I conducted an experiment on white mice to see if they would get skin cancer from tobacco. I distilled the smoke of cigarettes into a vile black paste and pasted it on their pink depilatoried backs. For the control, I used a known carcinogen, benzanthracene, I believe. I kept the cages in the cellar playroom of my family's home, tucked on top of the piano. All of my subjects developed lesions. I was a smoker at the time (a fact that did not favorably impress the fair's judges). After the fair, my biology teacher, also a smoker, helped me etherize my charges. And that's about the extent of my career as a scientist—a far cry from the lofty questions that had spurred my interest. The experience led, twenty years later, to the poem "Science," in which I began to discover the mythology of science as a guiding force in our civilization, a force like that of ancient gods, capable of generating both transforming hope and abject humility, a discipline that explores both the nature of reality and the nature of ourselves.

It is the mythological significance of science that continues to attract me as a poet, not simply the guiding stories and metaphors— "The Big Bang," "The Tangled Bank," and "The Neural Jungle"—but also the questions that drive scientific endeavor, the ambiguities and uncertainties it produces. No one with a television can fail to perceive that current scientific events play a prominent role in American culture, whether we understand the events or not. The incredible staying power of *Star Trek*, in all its combinations and permutations and spinoff subculture, attests to this. Where will those wacky intergalactic science nerds lead us next? But actual science events—news of research, for example, with the Hubble space telescope, the genome mapping project, biogenetic engineering, or the extinction of species—meets more than its share of the public's hostility and skepticism toward authority of any stripe. Today fewer Americans than ever believe scientists' warnings about global warming and diversity loss.

Their skepticism stems, in part, from the fact that to a misleading extent the process of science does not get communicated in the media. What gets communicated is uncertainty, a necessary stage in solving complex problems, not synonymous with ignorance. But the discipline itself is called into question when a scientist tells the truth and says, in response to a journalist's prodding, "Well, we just don't know the answer to that question."

The public's skepticism stems from other sources. Everyone knows all too well that an expert can be found (and paid) to take any scientific position that will support the claim of a special (likely corporate) interest. Coupled with this, the public is generally ignorant about the most basic science concepts. In a 1995 study fewer than 10 percent of U.S. adults could describe a molecule, only 20 percent could minimally define DNA, and slightly fewer than half knew that Earth revolves around the sun once a year. Lacking basic science literacy, one is unable to assess whether or not an expert opinion is persuasive. The capacity to appreciate such tropes as "the selfish gene," "punctuated equilibrium," "the greenhouse effect," or "cascading extinctions" is beyond hope.

What science bashers fail to appreciate is that scientists, in their unflagging attraction to the unknown, *love* what they don't know. It guides and motivates their work; it keeps them up late at night; and it makes that work poetic. As Nobel Prize–winning poet Czeslaw Milosz has written, "The incessant striving of the mind to embrace the world in the infinite variety of its forms with the help of science or art is, like the pursuit of any object of desire, erotic. Eros moves both physicists and poets." Both the evolutionary biologist and the poet participate in the inherent tendency of nature to give rise to pattern and form.

In addition to the questing of science, its language also attracts me—the beautiful particularity and musicality of the vocabulary, as well as the star-factory energy with which the discipline gives birth to neologisms. I am wooed by words such as "hemolymph," "zeolite," "cryptogram," "sclera," "xenotransplant," and "endolithic," and I long to save them from the tedious syntax in which most science writing imprisons them. As a friend from across the divide has confirmed, even over there the condition of "journal-induced narcolepsy" is all too well known. The flourishing of literary science writers, including Rachel Carson, Lewis Thomas, E. O. Wilson, Oliver Sacks, James Gleick, Stephen Jay Gould, Gary Paul Nabhan, Evelyn Fox Keller, Natalie Angier, David Quammen, Stephen Hawking, Terry Tempest Williams, and Robert Michael Pyle, attests to the fruitfulness of harvesting this vocabulary, of finding means other than the professional journal for communicating the experience of doing science. I mean, in particular, those aspects of the experience that will not fit within rigorous professional constraints—for example, the personal story of what calls one to a particular kind of research, the boredom and false starts, the search for meaningful patterns within randomness and complexity, professional friendships and rivalries, the unrivaled joy of making a discovery, the necessity for metaphor and narrative in communicating a theory, and the applications and ethical ramifications of one's findings. Ethnobotanist and writer Gary Paul Nabhan, one of the most gifted of these disciplinary cross-thinkers, asserts that "narrative and metaphor are more honest, precise and comprehensive ways of explaining an animal's life history than the standard technical format of hypothesis, materials, methods, results and discussion."

Much is to be gained when scientists raid the evocative techniques of literature and when poets raid the language and mythology of scientists. The challenge for a poet is not merely to pepper the lines with spicy words and facts but to know enough science that the concepts and vocabulary become part of the fabric of one's mind, so that in the process of composition a metaphor or paradigm from the domain of science is as likely to crop up as is one from literature or her own backyard. I subscribe to *Science News* to foster that process, not for total comprehension, but to pick up fibers and twigs, so to speak, that I might tuck into the nest of my imagination.

Here is a recent poem of mine that operates on this principle, a poem that pokes fun at some of the rather curious practices of my naturalist friends, while praising the deeper longing that motivates them:

THE NATURALISTS

When the naturalists
see a pile of scat,
they speed toward it
as if a rare orchid
bloomed in their path.
They pick apart
the desiccated turds,
retrieving a coarse
black javelina hair
or husk of piñon nut
as if unearthing gems.
They get down on their knees
to nose into flowers
a micron wide—belly flowers,
they say, because that's
what you get down on
to see them. Biscuitroot,
buffalo gourd, cryptograms
to them are hints of
some genetic memory
fossilized in their brains,
an ancient music they try
to recall because,
although they can't quite
hear the tune, they know
if they could sing it
that even their own wild
rage and lust and death
terrors would seem
as beautiful as the
endolithic algae
that releases nitrogen
into rocks so that
junipers can milk them.

I will leave the analysis, both literary and psychological, to the critics. What pleases me about this poem (other than the fact that I managed to use both "cryptogram" and "endolithic" in a single poem) is the way that an interesting fact (that rock-dwelling algae are a major source of nutrient for junipers growing in rimrock country) becomes a metaphor for inner, meditative aspects of the naturalists' work. As Leo Kadanoff wrote, "It is an experience like no other experience I can describe, the best thing that can happen to a scientist, realizing that something that's happened in his or her mind exactly corresponds to something that happens in nature." And so it is with poets.

But science and poetry, when each discipline is practiced with integrity, use language in a fundamentally different manner. Both disciplines share the attempt to find a language for the unknown, to develop an orderly syntax to represent accurately some carefully seen aspect of the world. Both employ language in a manner more distilled than ordinary conversation. Both, at their best, use metaphor and narrative to make unexpected connections. But, as Czech immunologist and poet Miroslav Holub points out, "For the sciences, words are an auxiliary tool." Science—within the tradition of its professional literature—uses language for verification and counts on words to have a meaning so specific that they will not be colored by feelings and biases. Science uses language as if it were another form of measurement—exact, definitive, and logical. The unknown, for science, is in nature. Poetry uses language itself as the object—as Valéry said, "Poems are made with words not ideas"—and counts on the imprecision of words to create accidental meanings and resonances. The unknown, for poetry, is in language. Each poem is an experiment to see if language can convey a shapely sense of the swarm of energy buzzing through the mind. The elegance and integrity of a scientific theory has to do with the exclusion of subjective, emotional factors. The elegance and integrity of a poem is created, to a great extent, by its tone, the literary term used to describe the emotional hue of a poem conveyed by the author's style. The aim of scientific communication is to present results to the reader, preferably results that could be obtained by another researcher following the same procedures; the aim of poetry is to produce a subjective experience, one that could be obtained through no other means than the unique arrangement of elements that make up the poem. Perhaps, among scientific specialties, the work of evolutionary biologists comes closest to that of poets, because its object of study (the biological past) is intangible, its method narrative: to tell the story of life on earth.

While the two disciplines employ language in different ways, they are kindred in their creative process. W. I. B. Beveridge, a British animal pathologist, has written several useful books about the mental procedures that lead to new ideas, whether in science, art, or any other imaginative enterprise. "Most discoveries that break new ground," he asserts, "are by their very nature unforeseeable." The process is not purely rational, but dependent upon chance, intuition, and imagination. He analyzes the part that chance plays by delineating three different types of discovery in which it is a vital factor: intuition from random juxtaposition of ideas, which is an entirely mental process; eureka intuition, which results from interaction of mental activity with the external world; and serendipity, which is found externally without an active mental contribution.

Random intuition links apparently unconnected ideas or information to form a new, meaningful relationship. It is like those children's books with the pages split in half. You combine a lumberjack's torso with a ballerina's legs, and—presto—a chimera is born. Eureka intuition is best represented by two classic examples. While visiting the baths, Archimedes suddenly awoke to a significant principle that would enable him to measure the volume of an object based upon the amount of water it displaced. At the time he had been wrestling with a royal problem. The ruler Hiero suspected that he had been cheated by the goldsmith who had crafted his crown. Archimedes' job was to determine the volume of the crown, so as to learn, from its weight, whether or not it had been made of pure gold. The Roman architect Vitruvius recounts the eureka moment of Archimedes' discovery:

> When he went down into the bathing pool he observed that the amount of water which flowed outside the pool was equal to the amount of his body that was immersed. Since this fact indicated the method of explaining the case, he did not linger, but moved with delight he leapt out of the pool, and going home naked, cried aloud that he had found

exactly what he was seeking. For as he ran he shouted in Greek: eureka, eureka.

The second classic example is that of Isaac Newton, who watched an apple fall from a tree and saw in its motion the same force that governs the moon's attraction to the earth. Eureka intuitions occur, Beveridge explains, when one "*seeks* random stimulation from outside the problem," and they "evoke the exclamation 'I have found it!'"

In serendipity one finds something one had not been looking for: an unusual event, a curious coincidence, an unexpected result to an experiment. The term was coined by Horace Walpole in 1754 after an ancient fairy tale that told of the three princes of Serendip. "They were always making discoveries, by accident and sagacity, of things which they were not in quest of. . . . You must observe that *no* discovery of a thing you *are* looking for ever comes under this description." Examples of serendipity are Columbus finding the New World when he was seeking the Orient, and Fleming discovering penicillin when mold accidentally grew on his discarded staphylococcus culture plates. For discoveries to be made by serendipity, more is required than luck. Beveridge emphasizes that "accidents *and* sagacity" are involved: one must be keenly observant, adventuresome, ready to change one's mind or one's goal.

I think of poetry as a means to study nature, as is science. Not only do many poets find their subject matter and inspiration in the natural world, but the poem's enactment is itself a study of wildness, since art is the materialization of the inner life, the truly wild territory that evolution has given us to explore. Poetry is a means to create order and form in a field unified only by chaos; it is an act of resistance against the second law of thermodynamics that says, essentially, that everything in the universe is running out of steam. And if language is central to human evolution, as many theorists hold, what better medium could be found for studying our own interior jungle? Because the medium of poetry is language, no art (or science) can get closer to embodying the uniqueness of a human consciousness. While neuroscientists studying human consciousness may feel hampered by their methodology because they never can separate the subject and object of their study, the poet works at representing both subject and object in a seamless whole and, therefore, writes a science of the mind.

I find such speculation convincing, which is probably why I became a poet and not a scientist. I could never stop violating the most basic epistemological assumption of science: that we can understand the natural world better if we become objective. Jim Armstrong, writing in a recent issue of *Orion*, puts his disagreement with this assumption and its moral implications more aggressively:

> Crudely put, a phenomenon that does not register on some instrument is not a scientific phenomenon. So if the modern corporation acts without reference to "soul," it does so guided by scientific principles—maximizing the tangibles (profit, product output) that it *can* measure, at the expense of the intangibles (beauty, spiritual connectedness, sense of place) that it cannot.

Clearly a divide separates the disciplines of science and poetry. In many respects we cannot enter one another's territory. The divide is as real as a rift separating tectonic plates or a border separating nations. But a border is both a zone of exclusion and a zone of contact where we can exchange some aspects of our difference, and, like neighboring tribes who exchange seashells and obsidian, obtain something that is lacking in our own locality.

One danger to our collective well-being is that language continues to become more specialized within professional disciplines to the extent that we become less and less able to understand one another across the many divides, and the general public becomes less and less willing to try to understand what any of the experts are saying.

Writing the Lowell lectures at Harvard in 1925, Alfred North Whitehead foresaw the dangers of specialization. In his work on the metaphysical foundations of science, *Science and the Modern World*, the mathematician cautioned that with increasing scientific and technological refinements

> the specialized functions of the community are performed better and more progressively, but the generalized direction lacks vision. The progressivism in detail only adds to the danger produced by the feeble-

ness of coordination ... in whatever sense you construe the meaning of community ... a nation, a city, a district, an institution, a family or even an individual. ... The whole is lost in one of its aspects.

The whole that we are losing is the belief in the integrity of life. We may have confidence in the earth's fecundity, its cleverness in reinventing life even after cataclysmic extinction spasms. But we are coming to suspect that the future of humanity is a detail that is at odds with the well-being of the whole. "If present trends continue," Beveridge wrote in 1980, "only about 1 percent of the Earth's surface will remain in its natural state by the turn of the century and a large proportion of the animal species will be doomed to extinction." Civilization is speeding up the process of evolution so fiercely that species counting on their genes to keep up lose ground as fast as we either claim or ruin it.

In addition to widespread species loss, the planet is experiencing widespread loss of cultures and languages. Jared Diamond, in a 1993 article, wrote that at the present rate of loss the world's six thousand modern languages could be reduced within a century or two to just a few hundred. He estimates that it takes over a million speakers for a language to be secure. The majority of languages are "little" ones having around five thousand speakers, and they are fostered by geographic isolation. The Americas at the time of the Conquest had a thousand languages; Diamond speculates that there may have been tens of thousands of languages spoken before the expansion of farmers began around eight thousand years ago. As remote regions become less remote, the little languages erode. Since each language represents not merely a vocabulary and set of syntactical rules but a unique way of seeing the world, these losses diminish our collective heritage.

Yet one can take some heart that specialized vocabularies within the large languages are burgeoning, and in no field are they doing so with more gusto than in science, providing fresh instruments for seeing the world. And, as Whitehead wrote, "a fresh instrument serves the same purpose as foreign travel; it shows things in unusual combinations. The gain is more than a mere addition; it is a trans-formation."

For both science and poetry the challenges lie in taking on the com-plexity of the most interesting questions (formal, technical, theoreti-cal, and moral) within our fields without losing connection with people outside of our fields. The idea of poetry with which I grew up was, I suppose, a particularly American one—that is, as an escape from the burdens of community into extreme individuality, a last bastion of rugged individualism from which one could fire salvos at an ever more remote, corrupt, and inane culture. Historically, how-ever, the voice of poetry has not always been construed to be the heightened voice of individualism. Among the original forms of hu-manity, art was unified with prayer and healing science. Poems and songs were manifestations of a collective voice, of spells and visions, of spirits returning from the dead. Such poetry transcended individu-alism rather than celebrating it. We may have gained much in terms of technical and artistic refinement through our specialized disci-plines, but we have lost the belief that we can speak a common lan-guage or sing a common healing song.

If poetry today needs anything, it needs to move away from its in-sular subjectivity, its disdain for politics and culture and an audience beyond its own aesthetic clique. A poem reaches completion in find-ing an audience. The challenge today is to reach an audience not com-prised solely of members of one's own tribe. We must write across the boundaries of difference. A poet finds a voice by holding some sense of audience in mind during the process of composition. It is one of the questions most frequently asked of poets: for whom do you write? And the answers range from writing for posterity to writ-ing for (or against) one's literary predecessors, from writing to an intimate other, to, as Charles Wright once said, writing for the bet-ter part of oneself.

I write with an inclusive sense of audience in mind, hoping to cross the boundaries that separate people from one another. I would like to write a poem that other poets would appreciate for its formal in-genuity, that scientists would appreciate for its accuracy in attending to the phenomenal world, that the woman at the checkout counter at Safeway would appreciate for its down-to-earth soul, and that I would appreciate for its honesty in examining what troubles and moves me.

The great biology watcher Lewis Thomas once raised the challenge:

> I wish that poets were able to give straight answers to straight questions, but that is like asking astrophysicists to make their calculations on their fingers, where we can watch the process. What I would like to know is: how should I feel about the earth, these days? Where has all the old nature gone? What became of the wild, writhing, unapproachable mass of the life of the world, and what happened to our panicky excitement about it?

And if science today needs anything, it needs to move out of its insular objectivity, its pretense that it deals only with facts, not with ethical implications or free-market motives. What science creates is not only fact but metaphysics—it tells us what we believe about the nature of our existence, and it fosters ever new relationships with the unknown, thereby stirring the deepest waters of our subjectivity. The critics of science are wrong in saying that because of its requirements for objectivity, rigor, and analysis, science has robbed us of wonder and reverence. The methods may at times be deadening, the implications spiritually and morally unsettling, the technology frightening, but nowhere can one find more sources of renewal than in the marvels of the material world, be they stellar or cellular. As Karl Popper put it, "Materialism has transcended itself" in unveiling mystery after mystery of process and velocity and transformation in even the dumbest rock.

The problem is the speed at which scientific knowledge is growing and the widening distance between those who have a grasp of that expansion and those who have not a clue as to its significance. During the past three hundred years, E. O. Wilson and Charles Lumsden point out, science has undergone exponential growth: the larger its size, the faster it grows. In 1665 there was one scientific journal, the *Philosophical Transactions* of the Royal Society of London; now there are one hundred thousand. In the seventeenth century there were a handful of scientists in the world; now there are three hundred thousand in the United States alone, and scientific knowledge doubles every ten years.

J. Robert Oppenheimer—theoretical physicist, head of the Manhattan Project that developed the first atomic bomb, opponent to the nation's postwar nuclear policy—was a man who had good cause to contemplate the ethical implications of scientific advance. In 1959 he delivered an eloquent talk titled "Tradition and Discovery" to the annual meeting of the American Council of Learned Societies, in which he spoke of

> the imbalance between what is known to us as a community, what is common knowledge, what we take for granted with each other, and in each other, what is known by man; and on the other hand, all the rest, that is known only by small special groups, by the specialized communities, people who are interested and dedicated, who are involved in the work of increasing human knowledge and human understanding but are not able to put it into the common knowledge of man, not able to make it something of which we and our neighbors can be sure that we have been through together, not able to make of it something which, rich and beautiful, is the very basis of civilized life. . . . That is why the core of our cognitive life has this sense of emptiness. It is because we learn of learning as we learn of something remote, not concerning us, going on on a distant frontier; and things that are left to our common life are untouched, unstrengthened and unilluminated by this enormous wonder about the world which is everywhere about us, which could flood us with light, yet which is only faintly, and I think rather sentimentally perceived.

Another point of contact: sentimentality is the enemy of both science and poetry.

I have in recent years been interested in the idea of the sequence, both as a poetic form, and metaphorically, as the word is used to describe both the life cycle of a star and the arrangement of genes within the chromosomes. The poetic sequence, as a contemporary form, aims for a kind of fragmented connectedness in a long series of poems or a combination of poetic lines and prose; perhaps it exemplifies the idea that within chaos there is an inherent propensity for order. My book, *The Monarchs: A Poem Sequence*, was inspired by the migration behavior of monarch butterflies and is an extended meditation on intelligence in nature and the often troubled relationship our species has with itself and others. This excerpt will stand as my evidence that careful examination of fact yields easily to contemplation of the miraculous, that a mode of questioning we associate with science can become a nest for poetic delight:

> A caterpillar spits out a sac of silk
> where it lies entombed while its genes
> switch on and off like lights
> on a pinball machine. If every cell
> contains the entire sequence
> constituting what or who the creature is,
> how does a certain clump of cells
> know to line up side by side
> and turn into wings, then shut off
> while another clump blinks on
> spilling pigment into the creature's
> emerald green blood, waves of color
> flowing into wingscales—black, orange,
> white—each zone receptive only to the color
> it's destined to become. And then
> the wings unfold, still wet from their making,
> and for a dangerous moment hold steady
> while they stiffen and dry, the double-
> layered wing a proto-language—one side
> warning enemies, the other luring mates.
> And then the pattern-making cells go dormant,
> and the butterfly has mastered flight.

In ecology the term "edge effect" refers to a place where a habitat is changing—where a marsh turns into a pond or a forest turns into a field. These places tend to be rich in life forms and survival strategies. We are animals that create mental habitats, such as poetry and science, national and ethnic identity. Each of us lives in several places other than our geographic locale, several life communities, at once.

Each of us feels both the abrasion and the enticement of the edges where we meet our habitats and see ourselves in counterpoint to what we have failed to see. What I am calling for is an ecology of culture in which we look for and foster our relatedness across disciplinary lines without forgetting our differences. Maybe if more of us could find ways to practice this kind of ecology we would feel a little less fragmented, a little less harried and uncertain about the efficacy of our respective trades and a little more whole. And poets are, or at least wish they could be, as Robert Kelly has written, "the last scientists of the Whole."

Mastery for human beings is no mere matter of being the animals that we are; we will always push the limits of what we are because it is our nature to do so. The human soul is an aspect of being that comprehends no boundary, no edge. And while the world's nature will always remain evanescent to us, no matter what we do to pin it to the page, we will always find new instruments, such as electron microscopes and literature, with which to gauge the invisible.

Recommendations for Further Reading

Aarseth, Espen J. *Cyberspace: Perspectives on Ergodic Literature*. Johns Hopkins University Press, 1997.

Abbot, Edwin. *Flatland*. Princeton University Press, 1991.

Barad, Karan. "Getting Real: Technoscientific Practices and the Materialization of Reality." *Differences: A Journal of Feminist Cultural Studies* 10.2 (1998), 87–128.

Barrow, John D. *The Artful Universe*. Oxford University Press, 1995.

Benedikt, Michael, ed. *Cyberspace: First Steps*. MIT Press, 1991.

Beveridge, W. I. B. *The Art of Scientific Investigation*. Random House, 1957.

Booth, Philip. *Pairs: New Poems*. Penguin Books, 1994.

Briggs, John, and F. David Peat. *Turbulent Mirror*. Perennial Library, 1989.

Bronowski, Jacob. *The Ascent of Man*. Little, Brown, 1973.

———. *Science and Human Values*. Harper and Row, 1965.

Buchanan, Scott. *Poetry and Mathematics*. Liveright, 1962.

Buell, Laurence. *The Environmental Imagination*. Belknap Press, 1996.

Calder, Nigel. *Einstein's Universe*. Viking, 1980.

Campbell, David G. *The Crystal Desert*. Houghton Mifflin, 1992.

Campbell, Jeremy. *Grammatical Man*. Simon and Schuster, 1982.

Carson, Rachel. *Silent Spring*. Houghton Mifflin, 1962.

Cohen, Jack, and Ian Stewart. *The Collapse of Chaos*. Viking, 1994.

Cole, K. C. *The Universe and the Teacup: The Mathematics of Truth and Beauty*. Harcourt Brace, 1997.

Courant, Richard, and Herbert Robbins. *What Is Mathematics?* Oxford University Press, 1941.

Darwin, Charles. *The Voyage of the Beagle*. 1936; Mentor, 1988.

Davies, Paul. *God and the New Physics*. Simon and Schuster, 1983.

Eiseley, Loren. *The Invisible Pyramid*. Simon and Schuster, 1970.

Fabre, Jean-Henri. *The Passionate Observer*. Ed. Linda Davis. Chronicle Books, 1998.

Ferris, Timothy. *Coming of Age in the Milky Way*. William Morrow, 1988.

Feynman, Richard. *Six Easy Pieces*. Addison Wesley, 1963.

Galileo. *Discoveries and Opinions of Galileo*. Doubleday, 1957.

Gleick, James. *Chaos: The Making of a New Science*. Viking, 1987.

Gould, Stephen Jay. *Ever Since Darwin*. W. W. Norton, 1973.

———. *Hen's Teeth and Horse's Toes*. W. W. Norton, 1983.

———. *The Panda's Thumb*. W. W. Norton, 1980.

———. *Wonderful Life: The Burgess Shale and the Nature of History*. W. W. Norton, 1989.

Griffin, Donald. *Animal Minds*. University of Chicago Press, 1992.

Guillen, Michael. *Bridges to Infinity: The Human Side of Mathematics*. Houghton Mifflin, Jeremy P. Tarcher, 1983.

———. *Five Equations That Changed the World*. Hyperion, 1995.

Harding, Sandra. *The Science Question in Feminism*. Cornell University Press, 1986.

Hardison, O. B. *Disappearing Through the Skylight: Culture and Technology in the Twentieth Century*. Viking Penguin, 1989.

———. *Poetics and Praxis*. University of Georgia Press, 1996.

Hawking, Stephen. *A Brief History of Time*. Bantam, 1988.

Hayles, N. Katherine. *Chaos Bound: Orderly Disorder in Contemporary Literature and Science*. Cornell University Press, 1990.

———. *The Cosmic Web: Scientific Field Models and Literary Strategies in the Twentieth Century*. Cornell University Press, 1984.

———, ed. *Chaos and Order: Complex Dynamics in Literature and Science*. University of Chicago Press, 1991.

Herbert, Nick. *Quantum Reality: Beyond the New Physics.* Doubleday, Anchor Press, 1985.

Hoffman, Paul. *The Man Who Loved Only Numbers.* Little, Brown, 1998.

Hoffman, Roald, and Vivian Torrence. *Chemistry Imagined: Reflections on Science.* Foreword by Carl Sagan. Smithsonian Institution Press, 1993.

Hofstadter, Douglas. *Gödel, Escher, Bach.* Vintage, 1980.

————. *Metamagical Themas.* Basic Books, 1985.

Holden, Alan, and Phyllis Singer. *Crystals and Crystal Growing.* Doubleday, 1960.

Holland, John H. *Emergence: From Chaos to Order.* Addison Wesley, 1998.

————. *Hidden Order: How Adaptation Builds Complexity.* Addison-Wesley, 1995.

Holub, Miroslav. *Dimensions of the Present Moment.* Faber and Faber, 1990.

————. *The Fly.* Bloodaxe Books, 1987.

————. *Intensive Care: Selected and New Poems.* Field Translation Series 22. Oberlin College, 1996.

————. *Interferron, or On Theater.* Field Translation Series 7. Oberlin College, 1982.

————. *The Jingle Bell Principle.* Bloodaxe Books, 1992.

————. *On the Contrary and Other Poems.* Bloodaxe Books, 1984.

————. *The Rampage.* Faber and Faber, 1997.

————. *Saggital Section.* Field Translation Series 3. Oberlin College, 1980.

————. *Shedding Life.* Milkweed Editions, 1997.

————. *Supposed to Fly.* Bloodaxe Books, 1996.

————. *Vanishing Lung Syndrome.* Faber and Faber, 1990.

Huxley, Aldous. *Literature and Science.* Leete's Island Books, 1963.

Kaku, Micho. *Hyperspace.* Oxford University Press, 1994.

Kant, Immanuel. *Critique of Pure Reason.* 1781; 2nd edition, 1787.

Levine, George. *Darwin and the Novelists: Patterns of Science in Victorian Fiction.* Harvard University Press, 1988.

————, ed., with the assistance of Alan Rauch. *One Culture: Essays in Science and Culture.* University of Wisconsin Press, 1987.

MacDiarmid, Hugh. "Poetry and Science." In *Selected Essays of Hugh MacDiarmid.* Introduction by Duncan Glen. University of California Press, 1970.

Messadie, Gerald. *Great Scientific Discoveries.* Chambers, 1991.

Nagel, Ernest, and James R. Newman. *Gödel's Proof.* New York University Press, 1958.

Nasar, Sylvia. *A Beautiful Mind*. Simon and Schuster, 1998.

Nelson, Lynn Hankinson, and Jack Nelson. *Feminism, Science, and the Philosophy of Science*. Kluwer Academic Publishers, 1996.

Newman, James R., ed. *The World of Mathematics*. 4 vols. Simon and Schuster, 1956 (especially the essay on Srinivasa Ramnujan).

Oppenheimer, J. Robert. *The Open Mind*. Simon and Schuster, 1955.

Paulis, John Allen. *Innumeracy: Mathematical Illiteracy and Its Consequences*. Hill and Wang, 1988.

Peirce, C. S. *Collected Papers*. 8 vols. Ed. Charles Hartshorne and Paul Weiss. Belknap Press of Harvard University Press, 1960.

Plant, Sadie. *Zeroes + Ones: Digital Women + The New Technoculture*. Doubleday, 1997.

Quammen, David. *The Song of the Dodo*. Touchstone Books, 1997.

Raymo, Chet. *Honey from Stone*. Hungry Mind Press, 1987.

Rukeyser, Muriel. *The Life of Poetry*. Paris Press, 1996.

———. *Willard Gibbs: American Genius*. Doubleday, Doran and Co., 1942.

Sagan, Carl. *Pale Blue Dot*. Random House, 1994.

Shlain, Leonard. *Art and Physics: Parallel Visions in Space, Time and Light*. William Morrow, 1991.

Snow, C. P. *The Two Cultures*. Cambridge University Press, 1998.

Steinman, Lisa Malinowski. *Made in America: Science, Technology, and American Modernist Poets*. Yale University Press, 1987.

Theophrastus. *De Lapidibus*. Oxford University Press, 1965.

Thomas, Lewis. *The Lives of a Cell*. Bantam Books, 1974.

Turner, Frederick. *Beauty: The Value of Values*. University Press of Virginia, 1991.

———. *Natural Classicism*. University Press of Virginia, 1992.

———. *The Rebirth of Value*. SUNY Press 1991.

———. *Tempest, Flute, and Oz*. Persea Books, 1991.

Watson, James D. *The Double Helix*. Mentor, 1969.

Whitehead, Alfred North. *Science and the Modern World*. Free Association Books, 1985.

Wilson, Edward O. *On Human Nature*. Harvard University Press, 1978.

Acknowledgments

Special thanks to Christopher Merrill, presiding spirit of this book; M. L. Williams, for encouragement and support; Barbara Ras, editor *par excellence*; and a host of others who contributed to this project in a number of small but essential ways: Roald Hoffman, Jim Finnegan, Roxanne French-Thornhill, Muriel Nelson, Tom Sleigh, Emily Grosholz, Jim Schley, Mark Rudman, Benjamin Paloff, William Corbett, Ben Vasali, Anthony Piccione, Judith Kitchen, David Sherwin, David Fenza, Doug Goetsch, Carlos Reyes, John Haines, Natalie Baan, Andrea Hollander Budy, David Biespiel, and Maurice Kenny.

The editor and publisher would like to thank the following for permission to reprint essays in this collection:

Kelly Cherry, "The Two Cultures at the End of the Twentieth Century: An Essay on Poetry and Science," reprinted from *Writing the World* by permission of the University of Missouri Press. Copyright 1995 by the Curators of the University of Missouri.

Contributors

The Editor

KURT BROWN is founder of the Aspen Writers' Conference and Writers' Conferences and Centers (WC&C). He is editor of three books in the Writers on Life & Craft series: *The True Subject* (Graywolf Press, 1993), *Writing It Down for James* (Beacon Press, 1995), and *Facing the Lion* (Beacon Press, 1996). He also edited three anthologies from Milkweed Editions: *Drive, They Said: Poems about Americans and Their Cars* (1994), *Night Out: Poems about Hotels, Motels, Restaurants and Bars* (1997), and *Verse & Universe: Poems about Science & Mathematics* (1998). Brown is the author of three award-winning chapbooks, and his first full-length collection of poems, *Return of the Prodigals*, was published by Four Way Books in 1999. A second collection, *More Things in Heaven & Earth*, is scheduled for publication by Four Way Books in 2002.

The Authors

KELLY CHERRY is the author of numerous books of fiction, poetry, and nonfiction, of which the most recent are *The Society of Friends*, stories (University of Missouri Press, 1999); *Antigone: A Translation*, Sophocles 2 (University of Pennsylvania Press, 1999); *Death and Transfiguration*, poems (Louisiana State University Press, 1997); and *Writing the World*, essays (University of Missouri Press, 1995). She is the Eudora Welty Professor Emerita of English and Evjue-Bascom Professor Emerita in Humanities at the University of Wisconsin in Madison and currently serves as Eminent Scholar at the Humanities Center at the University of Alabama in Huntsville.

ALISON HAWTHORNE DEMING is an associate professor of creative writing at the University of Arizona. Her books include *Science and Other Poems* (Louisiana State University Press, 1994), which won the Walt Whitman Award from the Academy of American Poets; *The Monarchs: A Poem Sequence* (Louisiana State University Press, 1997); *Temporary Homelands: Essays on Nature, Spirit, and Place* (Picador USA, 1996); and *The Edges of the Civilized World* (Picador USA, 1998), of which a chapter, "Science and Poetry: A View from the Divide," is excerpted and reprinted as an essay here. It has also been selected as a winner of the Bayer Creative Nonfiction Science Writing Award.

ALICE FULTON's most recent book of poems is *Sensual Math* (W. W. Norton, 1995). Previous books include *Dance Script with Electric Ballerina* (reissue, University of Illinois Press, 1996), *Palladium* (University of Illinois Press, 1986), and *Powers of Congress* (Godine, 1990). She was awarded a MacArthur Foundation fellowship in 1991 and has also received a Guggenheim fellowship and an Ingram Merrill award. A collection of essays, *Feeling as a Foreign Language: The Good Strangeness of Poetry*, was published in 1999 by Graywolf Press. She is professor of English at the University of Michigan in Ann Arbor.

FORREST GANDER holds a B.S. in geology, his first professional field. He is the author of four books of poetry: *Rush to the Lake* (Alice James Books, 1988), *Lynchburg* (University of Pittsburgh, 1993), *Deeds of Utmost Kindness* (Wesleyan University Press, 1994), and *Science & Steepleflower* (New Directions, 1995). He is also the editor of a book of translations, *Mouth to Mouth: Poems by Twelve Contemporary Mexican Women* (Milkweed Editions, 1993). He was recently the Briggs-Copeland Poet at Harvard University and is currently a professor at Brown University, where he directs the Creative Writing Program.

ALBERT GOLDBARTH is Distinguished Professor of Humanities at Wichita State University and the author of many books of poetry, including *Popular Culture* (Ohio State University Press, 1989), *The Gods* (Ohio State University Press, 1993), *Across the Layers: Poems Old and New* (University of Georgia Press, 1993), and *Adventures in Ancient Egypt* (Ohio State University Press, 1996). He received the National Book Critics Circle Award for *Heaven and Earth: A Cosmology* (University of Georgia Press, 1991), the Chad Walsh Memorial Award, and the Ohio State University Press/*The Journal* Award in Poetry. *Jan. 31* (Doubleday, 1974) was nominated for the National Book Award. He has also published three volumes of essays: *A Sympathy of Souls* (Coffee House Press, 1990), *Great Topics of the World* (Godine, 1995), and *Dark Waves and Light Matter* (University of Georgia Press, 1999).

EMILY GROSHOLZ is the author of four books of poems, including *The River Painter* (University of Illinois Press, 1984), *Shores and Headlands* (Princeton University Press, 1988), *Eden* (The Johns Hopkins University Press, 1992), and, most recently, *The Abacus of Years* (David Godine, 2000). A philosopher of science whose topic is reduction, she has authored a study on Descartes (Oxford University Press, 1991), co-authored another on Leibniz (Springer Verlag, 1998), and is at work on a book on the philosophy of mathematics. She is an associate professor of philosophy at Pennsylvania State University.

JONATHAN HOLDEN is University Distinguished Professor in English and Poet-in-Residence at Kansas State University, and the author of many collections of poetry. His book of essays and interviews, *Guns and Boyhood in America: A Memoir of Growing up in the Fifties*, was published by the University of Michigan Press (1997). His most recent books are *The Old Formalism: Character in Contemporary American Poetry* (1999) and *Knowing: New and Selected Poems*(2000), both from University of Arkansas Press.

MIROSLAV HOLUB was both poet and scientist. Born in Pilsen, Czechoslovakia, in 1923, he lived and worked in Prague at the Microbiological Institute of the Czechoslovak Academy of Science. A world-renowned figure, he was the author of seventeen books of poems, six books of prose, many translations, and over one hundred thirty papers on cellular immunology. He also served as editor for both scientific and literary journals. A survivor of two oppressive regimes—the Nazis and the Communists—Mr. Holub died in 1998 in Prague.

PAUL LAKE is the author of two poetry collections, *Another Kind of Travel* (University of Chicago Press, 1988) and *Walking Backwards* (Story Line Press, 1999). He has also published a novel, *Among the Immortals* (Story Line Press, 1994), a satirical thriller about poets and vampires. His essays on poetry have appeared widely in journals and anthologies. He is a professor of English and creative writing at Arkansas Tech University.

PATTIANN ROGERS is the author of many books of poetry, most recently *Collected and New Poems, 1981–2001* (Milkweed Editions, 2001). She is also the author of *The Dream of the Marsh Wren: Writing as Reciprocal Creation* (Milkweed Editions, Credo Series, 1999). *A Covenant of Seasons*, a collaboration with the artist Joellyn Duesberry, was published by Hudson Hills Press in 1998. In 1998, she received the Frederick Bock prize from *Poetry* and a fifth prize from the Pushcart Press.

STEPHANIE STRICKLAND's manuscript "V" won the 2000 Alice Fay di Castagnola Award from the Poetry Society of America. Her "Ballad of Sand and Harry Soot" won the 1999 *Boston Review* prize, and its Web version, http://www.wordcircuits.com/gallery/sandsoot/, was chosen for an About.com Best of the Net award. She is the author of *True North* (University of Notre Dame Press, 1997), *The Red Virgin: A Poem of Simone Weil* (University of Wisconsin Press, 1993), and *Give the Body Back* (University of Missouri Press, 1991).

DANIEL TOBIN teaches at Carthage College and the School of the Art Institute of Chicago. His poetry has appeared in many journals, and his work has received several awards, including The Discovery/*The Nation* Award and a Creative Writing Fellowship from the National Endowment for the Arts. His collection of poems, *Where the World Is Made*, was co-winner of the 1998 Katharine Bakeless Nason Poetry Prize, sponsored by the Bread Loaf Writers' Conference of Middlebury College, and was published by University Press of New England. He is also the author of *Passage to the Center: Imagination and the Sacred in the Poetry of Seamus Heaney.*

M. L. WILLIAMS's work has appeared in numerous magazines and anthologies, including *The Geography of Home: California and the Poetry of Place*, *Verse & Universe: Poems about Science & Mathematics*, *What There Is: The*

Crossroads Anthology, *Solo*, *The Prose Poem*, and *Quarterly West*. He is co-editor, with Christopher Buckley and David Oliveira, of *How Much Earth: An Anthology of Fresno Poets* (Heyday Press, 2001). He has taught at the University of Utah and University of California, Santa Barbara. He currently writes and lives with his two children in Santa Barbara, California.